A MAD WORLD, MY MASTERS

Commissioned and first performed in Silver ᵀ
Joint Stock Theatre Group, *A Mad World*
on the grand comic scale of the past tʰ
the present . . . The plotting leads
drunken doctor's office to a stri⟶   ⟶pon
look-alike to a last-act rendezvous   ⟶ingham
Palace' (*The Times*).

'Barrie Keeffe's *A Mad World, My Mas⟶   ⟶ght cracker.
Suggested by Thomas Middleton's 1608 ⟶ ⟶edy of the same
name, it has the gusto, delight in intrigue and feeling for low-life
exuberance of a Jacobean play . . . Interweaving these strands,
Mr Keeffe comes to the conclusion that those who tangle with
the upper class inevitably end up on their arse. But the play is
fuelled not by political anger so much as the blithe myopia of
true comedy in which people undergo any humiliation in pursuit
of an *idée fixe* ... I have seen few plays which plunder an old work
with such sparkish intelligence and wit' (*The Guardian*).

'The action tumbles throughout the theatre in generously
Jacobean proportions . . . The fun is fast, furious and complicated:
the evening sheer delight from start to finish' (*The Financial Times*).

'. . . what distinguishes Mr Keeffe is the ceaseless energy of his
plotting; the play never stops moving' (*The Observer*).

' . . . Mr Keeffe has written a boisterous, ribald and venemously
entertaining romp . . . His play unrolls like a roaring broadside
against our times . . . What is amazing is the way he manages to be
lunatically funny while at the same time constantly reminding
you that he has something serious to say — which could be summed
up roughly as "a plague on both your classes".' (*The Sunday Times*).

'Not since the heyday of Joan Littlewood have I laughed so much
at a modern carnival and been warmed so happily by its humour
and humanity' (*The Sunday Telegraph*).

by the same author

in Methuen's Modern Plays

BARBARIANS
Killing Time, Abide With Me, In The City

GIMME SHELTER
Gem, Gotcha, Getaway

in Methuen's New Theatrescripts

FROZEN ASSETS
SUS
BASTARD ANGEL

Barrie Keeffe

A MAD WORLD, MY MASTERS

EYRE METHUEN · LONDON

First published in 1977 by Eyre Methuen Ltd, 11 New Fetter Lane,
London EC4P 4EE
This edition 1980 by Eyre Methuen Ltd.
Copyright © 1977, 1980 by Barrie Keeffe
Set IBM 10pt Journal by 🅕 Tek-Art, Croydon, Surrey
Printed in Great Britain by
Whitstable Litho Ltd., Whitstable, Kent

ISBN 0 413 47410 0

AUTHOR'S NOTE

William Gaskill had the idea to make a modern Jacobean play, the sort of city comedy Thomas Middleton might write if he were still alive. He and Joint Stock Theatre Group asked me to write it. It was autumn 1976; it became not only Joint Stock's first comedy, but also mine.

I was set ten weeks in which to write the script after an intensive three week workshop period when the actors researched and created a number of characters which appear in the play, received crash courses in conjuring and talks from both police and villains on the art of the confidence trick. Verbal games of spiralling lies and experiments with Ben Jonson's 'humours' led to improvised comic scenes, sometimes inspired by a collection of newspaper cuttings on con-tricks that had led to court cases.

The storyline for the play suddenly clicked while I was reading a series of stories about the sale of Trafalgar Square to American tourists during the 1951 Festival of Britain and simultaneously listening to a radio programme about the (then) forthcoming Silver Jubilee Celebrations. We stole the title from Middleton (later a medium who had been consulted for purposes of research told us Middleton did not object, although he'd have preferred the play to be performed by a more prestigous company).

I don't think there is ever such a thing as a final script, but with this play it tended to change nightly: because it opened during the actual Silver Jubilee celebrations in London, lines were often altered to joke about an item in the evening newspaper. Usually the only actor alerted to the changed line was the actor delivering it.

All this contributed to make the play timely, but nothing dates faster than an 'up-to-the-minute' play. For subsequent productions in Britain, and especially overseas, some lines have lost all meaning; for overseas theatres, TV newsreader Angela Rippon and the Silver Jubilee Festival are distinct handicaps.

On occasions, I have worked with foreign directors tackling the play in an attempt to make it work for an audience in their theatre as it apparently worked for audiences at the Young Vic in the summer of 1977.

Whereas the changes made are sometimes quite drastic, in the case of the 1978 production in San Francisco, for example, they were minor. Apart from 'translating' some British slang to Mid-Atlantic, and Doc's Indian disguise Lime Pickle becoming a Chinaman called One Hung Low, the only substantial alteration was replacing Claughton's Angela Rippon fantasy with President Carter's faith-healing sister Ruth Carter-Stapleton; thus, Claughton's obsession for her began when he mistook her best-seller *Healing Hands* for a piece of pornography. The striptease scene took place during a faith-healing ceremony (to the disquiet of the theatre's landlords, a local church).

As I write this, the most drastic change is in Amsterdam where for the Centrum Theatre Rob Scholten, a translator who has the knack of so adapting my plays to Dutch locations and situations that not many people who see them realise they are British to begin with, is re-creating *A Mad World, My Masters* to fanfare Queen Juliana's abdication. This may require Claughton becoming the Queen's husband, Prince Bernhardt.

For companies considering altering or up-dating the text, the changes made for the Canadian première at the St. Lawrence Centre for the Arts, Toronto, in January 1980 are included in an appendix to this volume, as an indication of the revisions undertaken with Des McAnuff, with whom I had previously worked on a New York production of *Gimme Shelter*. His highly visual style owes as much to rock 'n' roll shows as theatre tradition; it was in stark contrast to Joint Stock's uncluttered and, by comparison, austere production.

In Toronto the Silver Jubilee Celebrations were changed into a fictitious festival to celebrate Britain's self-sufficiency in oil; this was suggested by the gasoline crisis in North America. Angela Rippon became Margaret Thatcher, since the play opened during the election campaign which saw the Conservative defeat, and a prologue was added and printed in the programme as an essential piece of setting-up.

To these revisions, some of Mr McAnuff's stage business has been added since his production seemed to work exceptionally well converting a play which was written for a small, in-the-round theatre into an extravaganza for a very large auditorium with an impossibly wide thrust stage.

I especially liked his opening 'con' in getting an audience not known to stand for God Save The Queen before a play to do just that. It involved playing enough of 'O Canada' until the entire house was on its feet before switching to Britain's National anthem.

March 1980.

A Mad World, My Masters was first presented by Joint Stock Theatre Group at the Young Vic Theatre, London, on 1 May 1977, with the following cast:

GRANDMA SPRIGHTLY, *a grandmother of Hackney*	Jane Wood
DOCTOR O'FLAHERTY, *a medical practitioner*	Tony Rohr
VI SPRIGHTLY, *a housewife and mother of Hackney*	Gillian Barge
BILL SPRIGHTLY, *a professional sportsman*	Robert Hamilton
HORACE CLAUGHTON, *a gentleman of The City*	David Rintoul
JANET CLAUGHTON, *a friend of the poor and needy*	Cecily Hobbs
MR FOX, *a gentleman of the press*	Will Knightley
RONALD SAYERS, *a superintendent of Scotland Yard*	Simon Callow
MR ROBERTSON, *a Trades Union official*	Paul Freeman
CHARLIE, *a minstrel*	Paul Freeman
ELIZABETH, *a most noble noblewoman*	Jane Wood
GUARD, *of Buckingham Palace*	Tony Rohr

Directed by William Gaskill and Max Stafford-Clark
Designed by Hayden Griffin
Lighting by Rory Dempster
Company & Stage Manager Alison Ritchie
Deputy stage manager Donna Rolfe
Assistant stage manager Alastair Palmer

Note: Robertson and Charlie should always be played by the same actor.

This production subsequently played The Round House, London and toured Britain. The Joint Stock Company was unchanged.

ACT ONE

Scene One

Before play: Music loud. Graham Parker's 'That's What They All Say' from the album Heat Treatment, as lights go up on Hackney Marshes, Sunday morning, very early. Enter GRANDMA beating her hands with the cold.

GRANDMA. I shouldn't be up this time of morning. Not at my age. I shouldn't be up, let alone out. No-one believes how old I am. 'Cause I've got me own teeth. Never cleaned 'em. Just rubbed salt in with me fingers. Now I don't bother. Seven o'clock on a Sunday morning, up here, at my age! Cold as a fart and the wind whistling round inside me corset. Never mind, never mind. Got on me long flannel drawers. Keep *that* warm and the rest of you'll be all right.

DOC enters.

DOC. Ah, morning to you Mrs Sprightly.

GRANDMA. What did you say?

DOC (*raised voice*). I said good morning.

GRANDMA. I'm hard of hearing. You should know — you're a doctor.

DOC (*shouts*). Good morning Mrs Sprightly.

GRANDMA. He told me six times I was hard of hearing. I didn't do nothing about it. I couldn't hear him.

DOC. Jesus in heaven preserve us. It's cold enough, bloody freezing.

GRANDMA. Bloody freezing.

DOC. I'll say —

GRANDMA. Pardon?

DOC (*loud*). It's bloody freezing!

GRANDMA. Learn lip reading they said. Why learn lip reading at my age? He said what I already know. I know everything that goes on round here. Rather read the back of me rent book than other people's lips.

DOC. I've never attended one of these before.

GRANDMA. What?

DOC. I've . . . never been to one of these before.

GRANDMA. I've seen hundreds.

DOC. This is me first time. I hadn't realised that it still goes on. An old sport, I thought.

GRANDMA. You got money for a bet?

DOC. Yes.

GRANDMA. In your pocket?

DOC. Yes.

GRANDMA. Keep your hand on it.

DOC. I will.

GRANDMA. As long as you've got your hand on it, it stays there. They're a thieving lot of bleeders.

DOC. Ah, right.

GRANDMA. If you keep your hand on it, to nick your money they've got to move your hand, right?

DOC. Right.

GRANDMA. If you find your hand's in a different place to where you left it, you'll know your pocket's been picked.

She has demonstrated this; she hands him back the wallet she's stolen. He smiles unsurely, checks its contents.

I like you.

DOC. That's a very nice thing to say, Mrs Sprightly.

GRANDMA. You're doing me son a favour. You're straight, I like that. If you're having a bent quack in on a job, for Christ's sake make sure he's straight, I say. You could make a fortune in Harley Street.

DOC. When they legalised abortions, the bottom fell out of my world.

GRANDMA. In Harley Street, the bent quacks are so straight they knight them. One got a knighthood for enlarging the prick on the Queen Mother's corgi, so I heard.

DOC. You're a foul-mouthed old bag aren't you?

GRANDMA. I can't hear when it suits me. Here they come, here they come.

DOC. You're sure that's them?

GRANDMA. Look at them, look at them . . . a bigger gang of rogues and villains would never be seen tramping the mud on a Sunday morning . . . Pakki bashers and handbag robbers and —

Enter two men with a sack.

GRANDMA. Let's have a look, let's have a look . . .

MAN. Here.

GRANDMA. Ferocious. Ferocious. That's a fighting bird right enough. O, that's a fighter. Look at the eyes.

DOC. Face like a plateful of mortal sins.

Enter ROBERTSON with a dog lead. He always smokes a pipe and wears a trilby hat.

ROBERTSON. Nye . . . Nye!

The men with the sacks panic, they turn their backs to ROBERTSON.

GRANDMA. It's all right, it's only Mr Robertson from the union. Hello there.

ROBERTSON. You seen my bloody dog?

GRANDMA. Don't let it loose round here mate. How's life?

ROBERTSON. All bloody go since we voted Heath out. There he is. Come on boy, come here — hey, leave that bloody poodle alone. Man with a poodle, my arse. Never trust a man with a poodle. Never trust a woman who wears hats indoors.

That's my philosophy. Here boy, here, come on. Good
morning Mrs Sprightly, keep the Tories out.

He goes. The men open the sack again.

GRANDMA. Open it up again. Eyes to scare the shit out of a
constipated nun.

MAN. Harry took one look at it and reckons your bird'll go under
in two minutes.

GRANDMA. Harry, he don't know a fighting cock from a bloated
pigeon.

Enter VI.

Hello love, how are you?

VI. I feel a bit lethargic, you know. Hello doctor. Pete's arf
getting fed up with that plaster cast on his neck.

DOC. Tell him to keep it on, for Christ's sake.

VI. Yeah, I tell him. It's by the door. He never goes out without
it. But he says it's strangling him.

DOC. Wait until the compensation comes through!

VI. When we get the money, we'll put it down on a deposit on a
house in Harlow.

DOC. After you've paid me fee.

VI. Of course, and the bent witnesses.

Enter BILL *carrying a sack. He dances round* GRANDMA
shadow boxing her.

BILL. Hello, hello —

GRANDMA. Morning Bill — you got it then?

BILL. What do you reckon then?

They look in the sack.

GRANDMA. Same weight, open it up — look at me then, you
bleeder, let me see your eyes.

BILL. I've had me eye on this one for a couple of weeks. On me
training run, down by Coronation Gardens, there's this

chicken run in the backyard. Daft cow didn't know it was a cock. Wondered why it weren't laying.

VI. Not like you then.

BILL. Watch it.

VI. Who you supposed to be fighting this time?

BILL. Some nignog from Birmingham.

GRANDMA. We going to start, or what?

BILL. Right.

GRANDMA. Got your money then doc?

BILL. The full equipment?

GRANDMA. Metal beaks and spurs, razors on their claws — tear each other to the bone . . . (*Laughs.*)

BILL. Right, bung on the hardwear. Excited, doc?

DOC. Ah, o — just, you know, concerning myself with the security precautions. A man in my position, you understand, can't afford to be seen in attendance of such a err . . .

BILL. Grandma, show him for Christ's sake. See for miles up here. There's Archie ready to do a clumsy three point turn at so much as a sniff of the cops and —

GRANDMA. Relax, look —

GRANDMA *takes* DOC *to one side to point out the security. The men are attending the cocks.*

BILL. You all right then sister?

VI. Just feel a bit lethargic, you know.

BILL. Still on the librium?

VI. No, he's put me on valium now.

BILL. Variety is the spice of life. How's junior?

VI. Crawling around . . . scares the life out of me . . . seventeen floors up . . . in case he falls out of the balcony.

BILL. Keep the door closed.

VI. I can't. It's suffocating. The central heating's on the blink.

Caretaker said it's hotter in our flats than it is in Majorca.

BILL. Keep taking the pills.

GRANDMA *and* DOC *are back. The men are laying bets.*

GRANDMA. You hold the bets, Vi.

VI. All right.

BILL. What we say, a score?

GRANDMA. I'm only an old age pensioner.

BILL. All right, we'll take your Green Shield stamps. What about the others?

VI. They'd be here if they was coming.

MAN. How about Harry?

BILL. Ah, see dad — our dad ain't coming this morning.

VI. Our dad ain't coming this morning, not this morning, no.

GRANDMA. This morning my son Harry — he is becoming a very rich man.

BILL. He's having his accident this morning.

MAN. A moody — on a Sunday morning?

BILL. Best time mate. He's going for the biggun, the jackpot, the number one pay-out. So better a Sunday morning — when there's not too many people in the docks.

GRANDMA. Harry's awarding himself a long service payment. For thirty years of slogging on the quays — thanks to the doc here's letter.

DOC (*with half a pint of Jamesons*). Like a drop? Then you don't mind if I do. (*He gulps from the bottle.*)

BILL. Terrible all these industrial accidents nowadays . . .

GRANDMA. The biggun, the king of cons. Be worth, let me see . . . your letter doc, saying he'll never be able to work again in his life . . . be worth twenty grand, I reckon.

DOC. Ah well, you get what you pay for. I gave him the letter meself yesterday. So as soon as it "happens" he can stick in the claim. Ah, well. (*Gulps again.*)

BILL. It is about to happen now. He'll get himself into position. Lay down right next to the hold. The hold cover will smash down beside him . . . dad'll let out a scream and writhe in agony —

DOC. I gave him a phial of ether to sniff . . . he'll be unconscious for a bit . . . in case their own doctor is on duty . . .

GRANDMA. And then . . . the big payout.

BILL. Got to help yourself to it, no-bloody-body else'll give it to you.

GRANDMA. Come on then. We here for the fight or just to get a draft up the Khyber pass?

BILL. Got the meat gran? Give 'em a smell of blood, give them a taster . . .

GRANDMA *produces some bloody dripping pieces of meat and lets the cockerels taste them. Then the birds are lowered into a pit. The men gather round, roar encouragement. From the pit feathers fly and there are screams from the cockerels, wing beats etc.*

GRANDMA. At him boy, at him.

DOC. His head's coming off.

BILL. This bird is a bloody chicken.

MAN. Looks like it's laying an egg.

BILL. At him — bloody have him.

MAN. He's going, he's going . . .

DOC. His head's coming off.

VI *sees* SAYERS *enter and stare at them. He wears a bowler hat.*

VI. Bill . . . Bill, Bill . . . I can smell a bogey.

BILL. What?

VI. I can smell a cop.

GRANDMA. You couldn't smell one if he stuffed his chopper

up your nostril.

VI. Over there . . .

She indicates SAYERS. *All panic and the two men run off.*

SAYERS. All right, all right.

DOC. Jesus and Holy Mary Mother of God.

BILL. I don't know where they come from Ronnie mate. I just happened to be passing and I saw these chickens going for each other and I was trying to separate them and take them to an old people's home for a treat.

VI. I come to feed the ducks. I thought someone had nicked the pond.

GRANDMA. I was stolen from me bed and bound and gagged and dumped here by foul smelling Pakistani illegal immigrants. I've only just set meself free.

SAYERS. Quite. I want a word with you Bill Sprightly.

BILL. I never seen them colour tellys before Ronnie.

SAYERS. I am afraid I have some bad news. In the docks at Tilbury, there has this morning been a horrendous accident. Your father —

BILL. O dad, poor dad . . .

GRANDMA. My favourite son, Harry?

SAYERS. He was unloading a cargo of spelter, I am informed. The hold cover blew down on his back. Crushing it.

GRANDMA. How tragic, how sad.

SAYERS. In crushing his back, the hold cover killed him — stone cold dead.

Pause, silence.

GRANDMA. Stupid bastard. Stupid pisspot son. He never could do anything proper.

They all exit. SAYERS *alone.*

SAYERS. Hello hello . . . hardly what you'd call grief with a large G. I smell a con. I smell it as surely as I smell a knocked off

car, a crooked log book. One previous owner? Who's that —
Julius Caesar? My wit numbs them to speechlessness. Then I
pounce with devastating questions to expose their guilt. Like
Magnus Magnusson I am. An intrepid interrogator. Twenty-
five years in the service, '43 murder cases. All that, and I still
can't get a mortgage. No home, no mortgage, that's me. I've
seen the places I want. Lovely little mock Tudor semis in the
wog-free suburbs. But these mortgage companies, they don't
want to know . . . Nor the councils. They say no, 'cause I've
got a police house. Look, mate, I've got nothing against these
Indians, Chinese, Pakistanis, Blacks you name 'em. I've got
nothing against them — apart from them being here. But
what I want to know is this — how come a Pakistani hot off
the banana boat can get a mortgage when a decent cop with
25 years service in the force cannot? Look mate, what this
country needs is someone to look up to.Someone to stop all
this weak kneed nancy pancying pussy footing soft balls
hard luck Jim have another large scotch. I went to
Northampton to try and get a mortgage. I heard they was
dishing out council mortgages left right and centre up there.
If you so much as parked on a yellow line they stuffed a
mortgage application under your windscreen wipers. What
did they say to me? O yes, you guessed it. (*He picks up the
cocks.*) I'll follow the Sprightleys. Observe them. From a
safe distance.

He goes.

Scene Two

Enter JANET *riding a bike and talking as she rides in circles.*

JANET. Janet Claughton the name. Crisis Intervention. I'm in
a hurry. Even on a Sunday. I'm always in a hurry. I'm a social
worker. Not enough hours in the day or days in the week or
weeks in the year for us. Not since the rise of the nuclear
family. Since the disintegration of closely knit working class
families with three generations occupying one residential
unit, the social problems have escalated.

She grins and cycles on. CHARLIE staggers on playing a trombone. He always has a joint in his hand and always carries a trombone.

JANET. Morning.

CHARLIE. What?

JANET. Good morning.

CHARLIE. What's good about it?

JANET. The sun's shining.

CHARLIE. Oh yeah. Good on you sun, that's a boy, keep it up. I'm going to the public baths. For a bath.

JANET. Jolly good, that's the spirit. Cleanliness.

CHARLIE. But they won't let me take the horn in with me.

JANET. Leave it at home. It's simple.

CHARLIE. Someone's stolen me home.

JANET. Good God.

CHARLIE. Last Thursday, I went out to buy a packet of cigarettes and a tin of Brasso and I got knocked over by a car.

JANET. Oh dear, how tragic, how sad, how shocking.

CHARLIE. I was walking across the road and it knocked me down. I went to hospital and when they let me out I went home — and it had been stolen.

JANET. How?

CHARLIE. The whole street, man. They knocked the whole street down.

JANET. If I were you, I'd call at Crisis Intervention.

CHARLIE. I thought I'd better tell the fuzz. Lost Property, you know. I've got to practise for a gig. I'm doing a big session next week.

JANET. Have a nice bath.

He exits playing the trombone badly. She cycles in circles.

That's exactly the sort of problem we have to face. At Crisis

Intervention. It's a new project set up by the council. Nissen huts, very Dunkirk spirit, on the carpark next to the town hall. I was just sort of hurled into Crisis Intervention. And people just pour into us, every minute of the day, and we have to solve their problems as best we can and it's only supposed to be a 36 hour week but My God sometimes I do 144 hours and I only stop then because I flake out, you know — collapse and you would not believe, honestly, how shattering it is on three phones and people pouring in and living off bacon sandwiches and Nescaff. Makes such a change to get away from it all. A quiet Sunday with mummy and daddy. Sundays with mummy and daddy have been especially quiet since mummy left home. For Eugene. Hairdresser. I told daddy it didn't take all night to have a cut and blow . . . He's a very important man, is daddy.

She parks the bike and goes to CLAUGHTON *who sits in a deckchair with papers on his lap.*

JANET. Hello daddy.

CLAUGHTON. Janet please silence, silence I say. I am a very important and very busy man. I am chairman of a consortium of property companies, a director of a £250 million insurance firm and I am especially preoccupied just now with Her Gracious Majesty's Silver Jubilee Celebration Committee.

JANET. Daddy, there's no need to stand up every time you say The Queen.

He has sat down, but stands immediately. He always stands to attention when anyone says 'The Queen'.

(*Shouts off*). Hello Mrs Herbert. What's for lunch eh? I'm starving, I could eat a horse.

MRS HERBERT (*off*). Chicken.

JANET. Chicken, yum yum. I met an incredible chap with a trombone on the way here and he said he went out to buy a tin of Brasso and when he came back someone had —

CLAUGHTON. Will you please be quiet Janet. This is intolerable. I am very busy. I have just bought 30,000 acres in Berkshire,

acquiring a window pane factory, a lavatory cistern manu-
facturers, seventeen blocks of offices and a motor components
firm. We wanted the motor components firm. I must decide
by tomorrow morning how to dispose of the rest.

JANET. Daddy, please don't tell me. (*Holds ears.*) That is asset
stripping.

CLAUGHTON. Nonsense. It is an exercise in efficiency expansion.

MRS HERBERT (*off*). Stuff it?

CLAUGHTON. I beg your pardon, Mrs Herbert?

MRS HERBERT (*off*). Stuff it?

CLAUGHTON. Stuff what?

JANET. The chicken, daddy.

CLAUGHTON. Damned woman. When there's a bed spare in the
geriatric ward I'll get an au pair . . . All right, coming Mrs
Herbert, coming . . .

He goes off.
Enter MR FOX, *doing a conjuring trick with a cigarette.*

FOX. Now you see it, now you don't.

JANET. That's jolly clever.

FOX. My card.

JANET. Mister Fox? How are you?

FOX. Well, at the moment, but unless I speak to Mister Claughton
I'll be in terrible trouble.

JANET. In which way — it says here you are a journalist?

FOX. I try to scratch a living. Scratch . . . geddit?

JANET. Terrific. But how can daddy help?

FOX. You're his daughter.

JANET. Yes.

FOX. Trattoria Bistecca.

Pause.

JANET. No, Janet.

FOX. Trattoria Bistecca Friday night?

JANET. You're losing me I'm afraid.

FOX. Never mind. Is he in?

JANET. He's with Mrs Herbert doing a bit of stuffing indoors.

FOX. I'll write that down.

JANET. What sort of journalist are you? You see, I'm terribly interested in perhaps trying to publish the special social study I've been making on bereavement.

FOX. You won't make much of a killing on that.

JANET. Perhaps New Society, when I get it finished, though goodness knows when that might be what with Crisis Intervention and —

FOX. Select any card. (*Offers a pack of playing cards.*)

JANET. What sort of journalism do you do? (*She selects one.*)

FOX. I am a gossip columnist. I spread scandal across six columns daily.

JANET. That's terrible. Why do you do it?

FOX. Twenty grand a year. Plus expenses. Put it back in the pack. Now I shall shuffle, tap it three times and darr dee dee darr. (*He produces a card.*)

JANET. No — the three of clubs.

FOX. Never mind.

Enter CLAUGHTON *triumphantly.*

CLAUGHTON. Janet, wonderful news, that telephone call then . . . who the devil are you?

FOX. My name is Fox. I'm a journalist.

CLAUGHTON. Ah city profiles, men who make our market tick — what what? I don't give interviews but since you're here, sit down. I began with not a penny more than £200 as capital when I had this bright little idea to —

JANET. He's a gossip columnist, daddy.

CLAUGHTON. Right, goodbye, I'm terribly busy just now, good-day, lovely to have met you.

FOX. Little question —

CLAUGHTON. I don't speak to scandal stirrers, I have no time for the dregs of vindictive, mischievous, Machiavellian —

FOX. Trattoria Bistecca Friday night.

Pause.

CLAUGHTON. Perhaps some beverage for Mister err . . .

FOX. A glass of lemonade.

CLAUGHTON. Janet, a glass of lemonade for Mister err . . .

FOX. Fox.

CLAUGHTON. Precisely.

JANET *goes.*

FOX. Lovely garden.

CLAUGHTON. Horticulturalist, are you?

FOX. I don't drink alcohol when I'm on duty Mister Claughton. It is still Mister Claughton and not Sir Horace yet?

CLAUGHTON. Not yet . . . ah, I have no idea what you're talking about.

FOX. A little whisper I heard.

CLAUGHTON. Rumours abound. Ignore them.

FOX. The girl you were with in the Trattoria Bistecca on Friday night . . . she was very young, very sexy. She wore a gym slip.

CLAUGHTON. Quite. An evening in town, half term, took her to the opera and then for a meal. Why not?

FOX. She was very young, the waiter said. He phoned me. He gets £50 a tip. Very very young.

CLAUGHTON. My —

FOX. Yes?

CLAUGHTON. My daughter. The girl in the Trattoria Bistecca.

FOX. Ah. Curiously, if you could help me here . . .

CLAUGHTON. In any way I can.

FOX. You being such an important and distinguished member of the city fraternity, on the Queen's Silver Jubilee Committee and — the waiter could not fail to notice that after the sixth Remy Martin, your hand had slipped under the girl's skirt and her knickers were lowered to her knees.

Pause.

Your hand, he observed, was rummaging around.

CLAUGHTON. She had an itch.

FOX. An itch?

CLAUGHTON. Perfectly ordinary itch. She asked me to lessen the irritation by . . . scratching it. For her. She could hardly have asked the waiter — after all, I am her father.

FOX. Why didn't she itch it herself?

CLAUGHTON. She was holding a knife and fork.

FOX. To drink Remy Martin?

CLAUGHTON. The itch had been irritating her for some time. She was unprepared to scratch it herself for fear that her hands may have been less than wholly clean, a consideration for hygiene that I find totally admirable.

FOX. But your hands —

CLAUGHTON. I was wearing rubber gloves.

FOX. In the restaurant?

CLAUGHTON. A perfectly acceptable practice. London is filthy this time of year. Right, good-day Mister Fox —

FOX. The taxi driver said —

CLAUGHTON. Oh God!

FOX. He said that in the back of his cab, he noticed you had opened her blouse and had your face pressed hard against her naked breasts.

Pause.

CLAUGHTON. That is true. I was . . . listening to her heart beat.

FOX. Why?

CLAUGHTON. I have a very sensitive ear. She was feeling unwell.
Quite straightforward for a father to —

FOX. He said you were sucking her nipples.

CLAUGHTON. I was administering to her — the kiss of life.

FOX. Why?

CLAUGHTON. Because she felt unwell, dammit.

FOX. Why not on her lips?

CLAUGHTON. She was blowing bubble gum and smoking. I
really fail to see, Mister Fox, in what way the health of my
daughter can possibly be of interest to your readers.

FOX. Mister Claughton, that girl was not your daughter. Why
the girl who I was talking to here —

CLAUGHTON. My *other* daughter.

FOX. You only have one daughter.

CLAUGHTON. Poppycock.

FOX. You do!

CLAUGHTON. Keep your voice down.

FOX. I checked, I checked in Who's Who. One daughter.

CLAUGHTON. Mister Fox, I am an extremely busy man and
unlike you I simply do not have the time to check such
trivial details.

FOX. You hardly have to check in Who's Who whether you have
one or two daughters.

CLAUGHTON. If she is not my daughter, then she is certainly
somebody else's. Good-day, Mister Fox.

FOX. Not until you give me a quote for my story.

CLAUGHTON. Fuck off.

FOX. With a double F?

CLAUGHTON. All right Fox, you little shit. What do you want?

What are you after?

FOX. A story for my readers. Your passion for schoolgirls. Man on the Silver Jubilee Committee, about to be offered a knighthood.

CLAUGHTON. Let us be frank and put our cards on the table, Mister Fox. You are a grovelling, snotty, pencil-licking little turd.

FOX. Yes, yes I'd go along with that.

CLAUGHTON. A dwarf, a parasite, a gossip mongering little farter who makes capital out of other's misfortunes.

FOX. I have to write seven stories every day.

CLAUGHTON. To write such a story would cause grave distress to my shareholders, my daughter, my mother, who has a severe heart condition, and to . . . dare I say it, the monarch herself.

FOX. You should have thought of all that before you fucked the bint.

CLAUGHTON. I call your bluff Mister Fox. Your newspaper's lawyers would hoot it off the page were you to attempt to write it. The word of an Italian waiter against the word of a man in my position? The word of some Yiddish taxi driver against the word of an English gentleman? You have no story.

FOX. Well, another time. I dislike men like you.

CLAUGHTON. The feeling is quite mutual.

FOX. I expect we'll meet again. Better story later, just before the knighthood, morning of the ceremony — oh yes. I'm on your tail, Claughton. There'll be other girls. Gym slips and —

CLAUGHTON. Mrs Herbert, unleash the hounds!

FOX. I'm off . . . lovely garden.

He goes. CLAUGHTON *is left alone.*

CLAUGHTON. Damn, blast. Little bitch, little blabbing-mouth whore, scrubber. (*He kneels.*) Arise Sir Horace . . . bless you,

your most excellent majesty . . . for this honour which I am
unworthy to receive . . . (*Rises.*) Damn. No knighthood for
Horace if any more little tarts start blabbing. Snotty nosed
journalist on the scent. Young girls . . . beautiful, firm
buttocked, nimble breasted, narrow thighed schoolgirls . . . I
renounce you, your dribbling lips shall remain closed to me
. . . until after Her Gracious Majesty has tapped my shoulders.
Get thee behind me, temptation . . .

JANET *enters with the lemonade.*

JANET. Has he gone?

CLAUGHTON. I sent him packing.

JANET. Daddy! Really, you have an erection.

CLAUGHTON. Nonsense, hernia playing me up again.

JANET. It's your winkle.

CLAUGHTON. Dropped a cigar down my waistband.

JANET. A stiff willy. What on earth have you been doing with
Mister Fox?

CLAUGHTON. Talking about Her Majesty the Queen. Any decent
loyal Englishman would experience a physical sensation at the
mere mention of her name.

JANET. Sometimes they don't even stand up for God Save The
Queen at the pictures.

CLAUGHTON. I shall go to the sauna and read the Telegraph.
(*He goes, with the deckchair and papers.*)

JANET. Poor daddy. Still pining for mummy . . . (*She goes,
taking the bike.*)

Scene Three

Church bells chime. Organ music.
BILL, GRANDMA, VI *and* DOC *enter with wreaths, which they
scatter around the grave.*

GRANDMA. He wanted to be cremated, Harry did. He wanted to

be cremated and have his ashes scattered over Upton Park when they was playing the Arsenal. So the ashes'd go in their eyes and blind the cocky bleeders.

BILL. Don't upset yourself grandma.

GRANDMA. He was my son. Strange experience to bury your nipper. He was a goodun. (*Weeps.*)

VI. Don't upset yourself grandma. We'll all miss him.

BILL. It won't be the same without him.

VI. Try to look on the bright side . . . he felt no pain.

GRANDMA. Yes, that's true. It was instantaneous.

BILL. Yeah, and it happened straight away.

VI. All them flowers. He was well loved by everyone who knew him. Street collection — they raised more than they did for the old age pensioners' Christmas party.

BILL. Yeah well — let's not hark back to that.

GRANDMA. You was a bleeder Bill — that money was for the old folks.

BILL. Give you half . . . poor dad . . . always a loser.

VI. I worshipped him . . . I idolised him. I wanted him at Kerry's wedding — the guest of honour.

BILL. Leave off Vi — Kerry's only eighteen months old.

VI. I did.

GRANDMA. I remember Harry wetting his bed like it was yesterday. Came through the ceiling and fused the wireless one night.

BILL. We'll all cherish our own memories of dad.

VI. I still can't get over the cruel twist of fate.

DOC. The hold cover, all ton and a half of it, it came smashing down before poor Harry was in the correct position, that is — out of the way. CRASH!

BILL. I thought Pete might at least have had the decency to put in an appearance.

VI. Pete went off to his auntie's on Canvey Island. In case there's an investigation and they find out about his neck. I miss Pete as well.

BILL. As well as what?

DOC. As well as can be expected. Ha ha. O, sorry. Want a drop — o well, don't mind if I do. (*Drinks.*)

BILL. I've been thinking . . . now when this compensation lark comes through . . . who'll be Harry's next of kin?

GRANDMA.
VI.   His mother/his daughter.

BILL. His son . . . all of us. You know what I'm going to do? I think I'll buy a farm with my handout. A ranch style bungalow farmhouse and I'll call it Harry's Hideaway — in dad's memory of course.

GRANDMA. Money won't bring Harry back . . . but just a grand or two for me. To see me off with a bit of happiness. What's a couple of grand to them — the upper classes? They write it off in cigar money every week. But with a couple of grand I could see the world before I go under. Soak me varicose veins under the Niagara Falls and get fucked by a couple of young, lithe Greek studs. They'll do anything for a bar of chocolate and an English cigarette.

VI. I'm thinking, if dad had got the money, he'd have given it to me and Pete and Kerry . . . for a deposit, on a three-bedroom, end-of-terrace house in Harlow, with an integral garage.

Enter CHARLIE, *staggering, blowing the trombone.*

GRANDMA. Show some respect, Mr Robertson.

CHARLIE. How do you know my name?

GRANDMA. The union —

CHARLIE. Ah, you're confusing me with my identical twin brother. He's very straight. No-one'd steal his house. They stole me home.

GRANDMA. Looking for a room are you?

BILL. We've got a vacant room now. Dad's.

CHARLIE. I had a very nice room. Then they stole the whole goddam street.

GRANDMA. That's not funny.

CHARLIE. Maybe I'll laugh about it . . . in about ten years. If I'm still here, and not . . . o, this is a cemetery. I need a fix. In the shade. I'm practising for a session. It's a very big session. I played for Dusty Springfield once. Whatever happened to Dusty Springfield . . .

BILL. Try under the graves marked S.

CHARLIE *wanders off.*
CLAUGHTON *is there, with a top hat and a wreath.*

CLAUGHTON. My condolences.

GRANDMA. Pardon?

CLAUGHTON. My condolences. I represent the docks board's insurance company. We handle their affairs in these matters. I speak on behalf of the entire board when I say . . .

Pause.

GRANDMA. We're very touched thank you much obliged.

CLAUGHTON. When I say, how deeply and inconsolably they regret this appalling tragedy which has immeasurably and irredeemably saddened and mortified all of us.

Pause.

GRANDMA. How much did he say?

BILL. He didn't — he hasn't got down to that yet.

CLAUGHTON. The post mortem revealed —

DOC. Ah yes, the post mortem revealed that Mister Sprightly suffered multiple compressed fractures of the cervical, dorsal and lumbar spine.

VI. I can't bear it, I can't bear it —

DOC. Had he lived, there seems little doubt that he would have had double incontinence and been quadraplegic.

CLAUGHTON. Quite, quite, indeed. In such grotesquely tragic

circumstances, compensation for the deceased's next of kin, whoever that might be, that compensation would have been substantial. Had he been working. However, since this . . . excrutiatingly obscene accident occured at a time when Mister Harold Sprightly's presence on the quay remains distinctly . . . mysterious, I regret that the unanimous decision of both docks board and insurance company is that we are able to offer only our deepest sympathy and . . . this floral tribute.

Silence.

BILL. Come again?

GRANDMA. I heard, I heard — you double dealing ponce. Mystery, mystery? There was no mystery — he was found dead on the job!

CLAUGHTON. What job, Mrs Sprightly?

GRANDMA. What job — why *his* job you snotty nosed upper class pen pushing procrastinating connivering pervert. He was doing his job like he's done it day in day out in all weathers with red raw hands and a breaking back for the best part of thirty years.

CLAUGHTON. According to all the evidence your son had not been allocated a shift nor signed on. Thus, ipso facto, he had no business being on the quay at all on Sunday morning last.

Pause.

GRANDMA. The stupid prat. He forgot to clock on.

BILL *(threatens CLAUGHTON)*. Now look here, I'm a fighter, mate. I've had nigbos the size of steamrollers slobbering at my feet.

CLAUGHTON. You know as well as I know — the deceased should not have been there in the first place. What precisely was Harold P. Sprightly doing on the quay at the time of the tragedy, hmmmm? Question number the second: an altogether more intriguing question. Why was Mister Sprightly on the quay when in his right had jacket pocket was found a letter from a certain Doctor . . . O'Flaherty saying that Harold P Sprightly was medically unfit to work through injuries sustained to his cervical dorsal and lumbar spine.

DOC. Benedictus benedictat Iesum Christum.

VI. What's that?

DOC. Latin prayer. For what I am about to receive on a plate may the Good Lord change the menu.

GRANDMA. What you're saying, you're saying — no payment?

CLAUGHTON. No payment.

BILL. No payment? But, Christ, he's dead — you're worth millions.

CLAUGHTON. That may be so, but the law is quite clear on this. That is the final decision good-day.

He turns to go.

GRANDMA. You git.

VI. Now now grandma —

GRANDMA. You reprobating fart-arsed apologetic snob — I'll kill you, I'll pull out your innards and eat 'em tandoori style. I'll make a skewer kebab of your balls and bury you alive you shit-house.

She lunges at CLAUGHTON *knocking him into the grave. She jumps in on top of* CLAUGHTON, *hitting him with her handbag.*
BILL *and* DOC *try to pull her off.*

BILL. For Christ's sake grandma, show some bleeding respect.

GRANDMA. My son would turn in his grave if he saw who I'm burying him alive with.

CLAUGHTON. Get off me, get off me. I'm drowning in your urine-stained drawers.

GRANDMA. My son wouldn't be seen dead with a dick like you here.

Enter SAYERS.

SAYERS. Okay, lads, all right — let's have some respect. A graveyard is the doormat to the kingdom of heaven.

CLAUGHTON. Officer —

SAYERS. Superintendent.

CLAUGHTON. Superintendent —

SAYERS. Superintendent Ronald Sayers, sir — in the force for
    25 years fighting the ever rising tide of crimes perpetrated by
    hardened criminals, vicious murderers, disgusting perverts,
    junkies, kleptomaniacs, rape merchants, embezzlers, queers
    (sorry, gays — we're all supposed to be liberal now, ain't we?)
    I've seen the shitty side of life, oh yes. In 25 years I have
    stared right up life's arsehole and I have not liked what I have
    seen. But never, ever, have I witnessed such disgusting
    desecrating disrespect for the deceased. And I've had 43 murder
    cases. All that, and I still can't get a mortgage.

CLAUGHTON. Superintendent —

SAYERS. I recognise you. You're Horace Claughton! On the Silver
    Jubilee Committee.

CLAUGHTON. Yes . . .

SAYERS. I've seen you after the police commissioner's balls.

CLAUGHTON. He and I play golf together.

SAYERS. Then allow me to help you out of the . . . ha ha . . .
    celestial bunker, if you'll forgive my whiplash wit.

CLAUGHTON. Thank you.

    SAYERS *helps him out.*

    Now look here. I do not wish to press charges. Clearly the . . .
    old shit-house there . . . was under some emotional strain.
    A momentary lapse of respect for the occasion and my . . .
    social standing.

SAYERS. The latter I noticed immediately.

GRANDMA. Press charges, press charges! I'm the one who ought
    to be pressing charges. Slander, lies, libel. Character vivisection,
    personality assassination. My son Harry hadn't clocked on you
    say. Listen mate, my son Harry was always in such a rush to get
    on with his job that he'd rush through the dock gates and get
    stuck in. He didn't even have the time to pick up his wages
    some weeks, he worked so hard. He didn't do it for money,

he did it for love of his country. He was too busy fighting on the quays the balance of payments deficit, mate.

SAYERS. He was a crooked little villain, grandma. The docks was just a tax dodge to camouflage his capers. Don't listen to her, your honour.

GRANDMA. Where's your sense of moral decency?

CLAUGHTON. Under the terms of my company's contract —

SAYERS. Your company doesn't happen to deal in mortgages?

GRANDMA. It's a moral question.

CLAUGHTON. There is no place in law for sentiment.

GRANDMA. Ahhhhhhhhhhhh, bastard.

She sits weeping. The SPRIGHTLYS *resuscitate her.*

SAYERS. Rod of iron, rod of iron — I admire that quality above all other qualities, sire.

CLAUGHTON. Not yet.

SAYERS. Pardon?

CLAUGHTON. I am not a knight of the realm, yet.

SAYERS. Only a matter of time, sir.

CLAUGHTON. You are a very perceptive policeman. You recognise quality when you see it.

SAYERS. Oh yes, sir. And men of quality, recognise I recognise their quality. I am discreet.

CLAUGHTON. A quality to be admired. I shall remember your name.

SAYERS. Then I shall write it down.

As he writes it down, CLAUGHTON *goes.*

Man of destiny that. The sort of man when, as he inevitably will, he takes his place in the Palace of Westminster . . . he'll prove to be the leader we need to become a great nation again.

SAYERS *runs after* CLAUGHTON.

GRANDMA. The mingy pox-scarred upper class cunt.

VI. Grandma —

GRANDMA. What?

VI. I just want to say . . . you do say such nice things. What you've said about my dad . . . has moved me more than anything the vicar said.

GRANDMA. There, there, girl. Don't cry again. There's enough rain in the heavens to keep the flowers growing without your tears.

VI *howls as enter* JANET *on her bike.*

JANET. Hello everybody.

VI. Are you family?

JANET. No, oh no. I'm making a study of bereavement.

VI. Well you've come to the right place here.

JANET. Janet, just call me Janet — social services Hackney.

BILL. We're a hard up case.

VI. And bereaved.

BILL. Look at her. She hasn't got a decent pair of carpet slippers and she could do with Meals on Wheels.

GRANDMA. Justice —

BILL. What?

GRANDMA. Justice, I say — justice.

BILL. What's she on about?

GRANDMA. I DEMAND *JUSTICE.*

Enter SAYERS.

SAYERS. Justice, Mrs Sprightly? You wouldn't recognise it if they spelled it out in alphabet spaghetti and strangled you with it.

GRANDMA. There must be justice.

SAYERS. Hello, I smell a con.

BILL. Mister Sayers sir — look. Someone's jacked up your Panda and nicked the wheels.

SAYERS. Bastards. Oi, you little bleeders, come back with them wheels . . . (*He runs off.*)

BILL. He said he smells a con . . .

GRANDMA. A con gone up the spout and no mistake. But at least it was a decent straightforward honest con. Just moral rewards for thirty years hard graft on the quays. But him . . . him . . . I wouldn't piss down his throat if his guts was on fire. (*Pause.*)

(*Inspired.*) To the union for justice!

BILL. A great idea! He did pay his dues, didn't he?

GRANDMA. Mr Robertson'll sort it out. You can't trust these connivering bosses, but at least you can trust your own class!

She and VI *exit.* DOC *is sitting drinking at the grave.*

JANET. Fascinating. The most extraordinary manifestation of grief I've seen! My special social study.

BILL. I bet you arf look sexy when you take your glasses off.

JANET. I can't see without me glasses.

BILL. You don't need to see when the lights are out. (*He does muscle building exercise.*)

JANET. Since the rise of the nuclear family, basic family units become isolated . . . where once it was three generations to . . . oooh, ah . . .

BILL. Feel that. (*His bicep.*)

JANET. Oh, I couldn't possibly.

BILL. Don't be shy.

JANET (*she does*). It's very . . . how would you describe it?

BILL. Like stainless steel.

JANET. Oh yes. You must be very fit.

BILL. I'm fit for anything. I'm a pugilist. I was schoolboy champion of England when I was 15. I have a great future.

JANET. Boxing? I hate blood sports.

BILL. Relax, you're all tense. You need a good massage. (*He massages her back.*)

JANET. I just don't have the time, ahh, ahh.

BILL. You see, I'm a professional boxer who . . . don't box.

JANET. I see. Sort of.

BILL. Allow me to explain. I train for fights. But I don't have them. Either me or the opponent, he cries off. Injured. So the promoter hands us both a pay cut for all the training what he thinks we've done but what we haven't done.

JANET. Well, that's a brilliant idea.

BILL. Like next week, there's this darkie up in Birmingham. Eight rounder. Only he's going to 'mysteriously' injure his ankle a day before the fight. Then we share out. Good bloke is Winston — good bloke.

JANET. Jolly good.

DOC *goes to* BILL.

DOC (*gulping from a flask*). My nerves, you understand . . . just a question of what we call in the trade . . . palpitating nervosity. Remedy here. (*Gulps.*) Don't mind if I do? Good, quite right. You see Billy boy, what has occurred to me is the fact that . . . what has crossed my mind is the notion that . . . there is a slight peculiarity here.

BILL. Too fucking right.

DOC. The peculiarity that . . . the irregularity that . . . on the deceased . . . they found a letter describing in total detail the accident . . . before the fucking accident happened.

Pause, gulps.

O my God.

Pause.

BILL. Tell them you're psychic.

DOC. Do you think it'd convince them?

BILL. No chance.

DOC. I must get the bloody letter back before he realises the full implications . . .

BILL. Hang about, hang about . . . don't panic. Now . . . what'll happen is . . . they'll come to you . . . to investigate.

DOC. So what'll I do?

BILL. Wait. Don't rush things . . . await the moment they pounce and then . . . smash back.

DOC. I'll do that.

BILL. And while you're about it, this Birmingham bloke — Winston Kershaw — can you write him a letter saying he's done his ankle and has got to cry off the fight?

DOC. How much?

BILL. Twenty quid.

DOC. Make it thirty.

BILL. Fifteen and two bottles of Johnny Walker Black Label.

DOC. Make sure they're real — no more bloody vinegar.

BILL. Right.

DOC. God, I strike a hard bargain. Ban the pill — I'm a bloody abortionist not a con man.

DOC *exits.*
SAYERS *enters.*

SAYERS. You got your motor?

BILL. The tax is in the post.

SAYERS. I need a bloody lift — bastards nicked me wheels.

BILL. I'm on a training run . . .

SAYERS. Drop me off at the station.

BILL. I'm giving the lady a lift home.

SAYERS. She's got a bike.

BILL. You can borrow it.

BILL *and* JANET *exit.* SAYERS *goes to the bike.*

SAYERS. First time I've put my arse to a chopper.

CHARLIE *staggers on, the trombone hanging by a strap on his back.*

Hello hello — what have we here.

CHARLIE. I ain't got no home to go to.

SAYERS. No fixed abode.

CHARLIE. Someone stole it.

SAYERS. Who?

CHARLIE. The GLC, I think.

SAYERS. Come off it, mate. Don't try that on me or you'll get a bunch of cell keys rattled around your teeth. Right, no fixed abode, arms like pin cushions and no job I dare say.

CHARLIE. I had a job. I played the horn on a Dusty Springfield disc. (*He beckons* SAYERS, *then says in his ear:*) You Don't Have To Say You Love Me. That was in 1966. I blew so beautifully . . . (*He falls to his knees.*) . . . I have never felt I could re-reach the heights I attained. I guess you could call me a perfectionist. (*Falls flat on his face.*)

SAYERS. You don't look like one. You'd better come with me — a night in the cells, sober you up. (*He picks him up.*)

CHARLIE. Whatever happened to Dusty Springfield?

SAYERS *leads off* CHARLIE *in a half-Nelson.*

Scene Four

Music loud: first verse of Dusty Springfield's You Don't Have To Say You Love Me.
It fades as JANET *enters, heaping piles of reports and tatty books into a tatty briefcase. She is wearing a gymslip.*

JANET. I have nightmares about my cases. Faces keep looming at me in my sleep saying — 'Where's the radio you promised me, where's my rent rebate, where's my accommodation, what about my Meals on Wheels last Wednesday'. They reckon after

about three months in Crisis Intervention you have to get out.
I haven't even had time to buy a proper dress. Good job I
keep the old Benenden gear in the office. . . . I was there at the
same time as Princess Anne . . . oh a right little stuck up madam
she was . . . I was heavily into the cultural revolution but I just
couldn't get through to Annie . . . well, it's a lovely day for
it . . . mayor's planting a tree here in the park . . . to
commemorate the Silver Jubilee or something . . . I've been
pushed out to represent social services . . . (*At bike.*) Oh
drat . . . another puncture . . . can't leave the bike unattended
for five minutes without someone letting down the tyres . . .

*She bends to look at the puncture. Her knickers revealed,
arse in the air, as* CLAUGHTON *enters. He sees it.*

CLAUGHTON. Good God. Such innocence, such nonchalant . . .
stirrings inside her . . . and she doesn't know what they are.
My sweet young precious little child. Ah, little one, to rub
my aged palm across such firm little buttocks, to feel the taut
white cotton straining against the full firm voluptuousness
of . . .

JANET. I can feel someone looking at me . . . daren't turn round.

CLAUGHTON (*behind her*). Little one . . . relax, unwind, don't
be . . .

He touches her arse. She leaps and turns.

JANET. Daddy!

CLAUGHTON. Janet. Why are you wearing those clothes?

JANET. Why were you touching my arse?

CLAUGHTON. A slight . . . a sudden sharp stabbing pain in my
chest . . . I was about to fall . . . I stretched out my hand to
break the fall and it seems to have connected with your . . .
bottom. Better now, oh yes, I'm all right now.

JANET. Daddy, you have an erection.

CLAUGHTON. Nonsense. It's my electronic calculator.

JANET. In your trousers?

CLAUGHTON. A precaution against pickpockets.

JANET. O do let me borrow it. One of my clients brought in her son's homework — a mathematical problem, I said I'd do it for him.

CLAUGHTON. Mental arithmetic, excellent — fire away.

JANET. Well, a train has 351 passengers and at the first station it stops and 6 get off and 17 get on and at the next station 31 get off and 14 and a dog get on and at the next station the dog and 33 get off and 27 get on and at the next station 7 get off and 5 get on —

CLAUGHTON. Yes, yes, go on?

JANET. How many stations did the train stop at?

CLAUGHTON. Yes, well. Mustn't hold you up.

JANET. See you next Sunday daddy. The mayor's planting a tree.

CLAUGHTON. Wonderful.

She goes. He wipes his forehead.

Pull yourself together Claughton. By God, that was close.

SAYERS (*who has entered*). It was indeed sir.

CLAUGHTON. Not yet.

SAYERS. Just a matter of time.

CLAUGHTON. As a matter of fact, not so long ago. I have received a call from the Palace asking whether I would consider a knighthood. I said — I would.

SAYERS. Let me be the first to congratulate you, sire. (*He falls to his knees and bows.*)

CLAUGHTON. Thank you. But, must resist temptation. Renounce the evils of puberty flesh. Get thee behind me Satan.

SAYERS. This close enough sir?

CLAUGHTON. You fool. I shall not succumb, I shall not succumb.

SAYERS. I was thinking sir, none of my business — but these young schoolgirls . . . could handicap honours . . . medical attention, sir. A few erection dampening pills. To take when lust throbs through your arteries.

CLAUGHTON. Excellent, superintendent.

SAYERS. And . . . I wouldn't risk Harley Street quacks, sir. Lest word gets out. An out-of-the-way doctor, I think would be best.

CLAUGHTON. Hmm. Perhaps you're right. I foresee a great future for you superintendent. I shall remember your name.

SAYERS. Then I shall write it down.

CLAUGHTON goes. FOX has entered.

There's a man to be reckoned with. You can tell he's pure stock, pure English. A man of destiny. (*He burps.*) I can sense it. (*Exits.*)

FOX. Incest in suburbia? Not a bad yarn had it been consummated. If Claughton was a Roman centurion they'd have called him Coitus Interruptus.

He begins a trick: turns a Union Jack handkerchief into a coin, during –

Never mind, time's on my side. I can wait. At school I'd hide a kipper behind a radiator before the summer break. I could wait till autumn for the stench. Claughton is my fish. As long as there are politicians, there'll be corruption. As long as there are bishops, there'll be choirboys. As long as men have ambitions, and whores have cunts, I'll fill my seven columns every day.

The trick completed, he spins the coin and goes.

Scene Five

Betting shop race result announcement.
GRANDMA *and* BILL *enter, listen, tear up betting slips.*

BILL. Can't win them all grandma.

ROBERTSON *enters.*

You all right – found a room?

GRANDMA. What you talking about? That's Mr Robertson from the union who we've come to see.

ROBERTSON. You're confusing me with my identical twin brother, the drugged up layabout. They've let him out again, have they?

BILL. He was playing the trombone in the cemetery.

ROBERTSON. Typical. No respect for anyone or anything. Right embarrassment to me — union official, doing me best to keep the status quo and —

BILL. We went to the union headquarters and the frizzy haired bint with the green nail varnish and the tits hanging round her knees said you're the one to collar. She said you'd sort it out without animosity or rancour.

ROBERTSON. Without what?

GRANDMA. Animosity or rancour.

ROBERTSON. Then that'll be me she's talking about.

GRANDMA. Mr Robertson, we want your help. You heard about the outrage, the travesty of justice, the double dealing and collusion, the duplicity?

ROBERTSON. Yes, yes — I have been informed of what transpired following the accident.

GRANDMA. So what are you going to do about it?

ROBERTSON. Ah yes, well — quite, precisely.

Another race result.

ALL. Fuck it. (*They tear up slips.*)

GRANDMA. We've come to you for justice.

ROBERTSON. Justice eh, it's to be justice, is it?

GRANDMA. We want you and the union to take our case to the highest courts in the land. Fight dirty if necessary.

ROBERTSON. A woman of passion, eh — that you?

GRANDMA. That's me.

ROBERTSON. Well, quite frankly, there is no doubt in my mind and I'm speaking off the record here, you understand, but there is no doubt in my mind that the authorities are sailing pretty bloody close to the wind.

GRANDMA. Whip it up then. Bring the whole country to a
standstill — the national strike all over again. Make them bleed
for the day they denied the Sprightlys.

ROBERTSON. Look, err, the first question we must ask is — are
we standing on firm ground.

BILL. What do you mean, Mister Robertson?

ROBERTSON. Let's not shilly shally. We've got to be realistic.

BILL. We've come to you for help. We're the same class, we're on
the same side, we're loyal.

ROBERTSON. There's no question about anyone's loyalties.
But . . . I've read the authorities' reports and it does seem
pretty clear to me that some of the essential issues are, to say
the least, somewhat blurred.

BILL. Blurred?

ROBERTSON. The basic issue being, your son wasn't at work
when the tragedy happened.

GRANDMA. Not at work? If he weren't at work, he'd be alive
today.

ROBERTSON. Work I mean in the sense of working.

GRANDMA. He was on the quay unloading.

ROBERTSON. He hadn't clocked on.

GRANDMA. He —

ROBERTSON. He hadn't clocked on, he hadn't started a shift,
so he wasn't getting paid so he wasn't working.

GRANDMA. You can work without getting paid.

ROBERTSON. Rubbish. Work means getting paid. You can get
paid for doing nothing and, officially, be classified as working.
But you cannot work without getting paid and be officially
classified as working. Be realistic. Mustn't sift the greens too
much. Got to know when to leave off.

BILL. Leave off, we haven't started yet. Shall I lip him gran,
shall I give him a right hook up his hooter?

ROBERTSON. Oh yes, the Hackney light middleweight champion
— when's your next fight?

BILL. Shoreditch Town Hall June 1st.

ROBERTSON. You couldn't box kippers. I am sorry Mrs Sprightly.
I've been through all the bumf on this case. Like all the bumf
Transport House churn out every day. I'm up to here with
bumf. Union man for 30 years, official here for 14. Labour
party all me life. Used to be the party of reform when I started,
and I used to be an optimist. Can't risk any more of the
credibility of the movement for your Harry's . . . irregularity.

GRANDMA. I don't understand . . . we're on the same side.

ROBERTSON. I wouldn't give you tuppence for your case
Mrs Sprightly. I'm sorry. That's the way it is now. These
bloody city slickers, high finance, the whole root of the
country's problems. And the young Trots like my bloody son.
O, he's got his heart in the right place — wants to change the
world. But what I say to him is this: How are you going to
get 25 million workers to follow you? He's got as much chance
as you have of winning your case. Well, seem to have settled
all this without animosity or rancour.

GRANDMA. I'm not taking this lying down —

ROBERTSON. That's what my missus says. (*Laughs*.) Next
election, there'll be the biggest fucking Tory landslide there's
ever been. (*Goes*.)

GRANDMA. That Robertson — sold out to the bosses, I want
revenge. And the money, twenty grand Harry was entitled to.
I want revenge! And that Claughton bloke from the insurance
company, that snob . . . We'll get him.

BILL. But how will we do that?

GRANDMA. I didn't tumble him in the grave for nothing.
Fingered his pocket —

BILL. What'd you get?

GRANDMA. Letter . . . from Buckingham Palace about he's up
for a knighthood. Got his address.

BILL. Fantastic, you thieving old cow. I'll have a little shifty in his place, suss it out — find out about him.

GRANDMA. That's the spirit. Horace Claughton, can you hear me? You will tremble at the name, Sprightly!

They go.

Scene Six

CLAUGHTON *enters.*

CLAUGHTON. I demand to see a doctor. I have been waiting three minutes and 25 seconds.

Enter DOC.

DOC. Who's next?

CLAUGHTON. I am.

DOC. O God. Would you like a drink? Then you don't mind if I do. (*Gulps.*)

CLAUGHTON. We have met before.

DOC. O no, definitely not.

CLAUGHTON. You are Doctor O'Flaherty?

DOC (*adopts an Indian accent*). No, no no sir. Not Doctor O'Flaherty. A lot of people tell me I bear an astonishing facial resemblance to a certain Irish Doctor, but I am not him.

CLAUGHTON. The name on the brass plaque outside says Doctor O'Flaherty.

DOC. That is perfectly correct. You see, when I first arrived in the British Isles, my colleagues told me in this vicinity there were hostilities towards Indians, so I adopted an Irish name. My real name is . . .

Pause.

CLAUGHTON. What?

DOC. Tandoori . . . Shamee Kebab . . . Popadom. My friends call me Lime Pickle.

CLAUGHTON. I see. Well doctor, anonymity is what I crave. I am here in Hackney on an . . . irregular mission.

DOC. You have the letter with you?

CLAUGHTON. What letter?

DOC. About the accident?

CLAUGHTON. Doctor Popadom, I have not mentioned any letter about an accident.

DOC. Ah, part of my training in Calcutta. A guru aroused my powers of extra sensory perception.

CLAUGHTON. Poppycock.

DOC. No, Popadom. Mister Claughton — I see around you an aura of great tension. You must relax.

CLAUGHTON. I do not have time to relax. I am a very important man. I am a big cheese in the City and organising the Silver Jubilee celebrations for the Queen.

DOC. Good God.

CLAUGHTON. Doctor, that is part of my problem.

DOC. It's standing up.

CLAUGHTON. I know it's standing up. I'm terrified of sitting down lest it stands up.

DOC. Why is it standing up?

CLAUGHTON. Please doctor . . . help me . . . some pills, some embalming lotion to . . . stop it standing up when I don't want it to stand up.

DOC. Yes, yes, but — I do not understand what could have aroused it?

CLAUGHTON. I mentioned . . . Her Gracious Majesty the Queen.

DOC. O dear dear dear. Is that the only time it stands up?

CLAUGHTON. In absolute confidence.

DOC. Oh yes.

CLAUGHTON. In achieving all I have achieved, in striving for all I have secured, I feel as though a great segment of my life, the ordinary simple pleasures lesser mortals take for granted . . . has passed me by. I long for the innocence of childhood, perhaps that is what so lustfully attracts me towards young schoolgirls.

DOC. They're not innocent. They're the biggest prick teasers in the world.

CLAUGHTON. My delusion. I want to plunge headlong into innocence, I am enthralled by their sweet beauty, it will destroy me. Help my irrational lust, please, please.

Pause.

DOC. I think I can help you.

CLAUGHTON. Thank you, Lime Pickle.

DOC. What you must do is . . . transfer your irrational lust to . . . a being out of your reach. An object —

CLAUGHTON. I'm not fucking no tables.

DOC. A person, oh yes. Is there someone you like especially on television?

CLAUGHTON. I only watch the news. Ah . . . (*His face is full of joy.*)

DOC. Excellent. The personification of two passions.

CLAUGHTON. You have been very helpful, Doctor.

DOC. Part of the service. And, err . . . some sleeping pills, to help you sleep.

CLAUGHTON. Good-day sir. You will forget I came.

DOC. Of course.

CLAUGHTON *goes handing the doctor a £20 note.* DOC *swigs frenziedly at the flask. He turns,* FOX *is standing there.*

Are you next?

FOX. No, I was waiting for a friend . . . he seems to have gone. (*Goes out.*)

DOC. Jesus, Holy Mary, Mother of God. (*Drinks.*) I shouldn't be farting about like this. Not a man of my professional standing. I shouldn't be at the beck and call of all and sundry.

Night after night, waiting-room full like a rush hour bus.
Stupid grinning expectant mothers, cancer carcasses with
pleading eyes, TB merchants, gobbing on me threadbare lino,
methys warming their stinking feet on me radiator. And buggers
with piles hanging like bunches of grapes. (*Drinks.*) Every night.
I put everyone of the bastards on valium. I missed me chance. I
should have cleaned up on the abortion racket. I should have
the gin and corkscrew grannies out of business. The Pope must
take on the heathen and the Prods and fight the evil pill.
(*Drinks.*) I didn't spend seven years at Trinity for a life like
this. The Jamesons'll kill me. Worse way to die. I must tell
old ma Sprightly about Claughton's visit. He doesn't know
the sleeping pills I gave him are really aphrodisiacs. (*Laughs.*)
For a service like that she'll get me fucking letter back. (*Goes.*)

Scene Seven

JANET *enters, sets the TV.* CHARLIE *enters playing the trombone
very badly.*

CHARLIE. I just . . . can't do it anymore, Janet.

JANET. It sounded very nice to me.

CHARLIE. Dusty Springfield said I blew the best horn in Hackney.
(*Rolls a joint.*)

JANET. I loved that record.

CHARLIE. It was my last session. I feel all washed up. But I got
this gig you see. I took this job. They didn't know what had
happened to me . . .

JANET. You must fight the addiction, Charlie — you must fight
it. I'll help you.

CHARLIE. On Wednesday June 1st a session in the studio. It's me
big comeback.

JANET. That's wonderful news.

CHARLIE. It'll be the first time the Sex Pistols have used brass.

JANET. Well time rushing on . . . don't let me hold you up. Let's go and find out about the dormitory.

CHARLIE. I don't want to sleep with Aunt Sally, Janet. I want my home back. (*Goes.*)

Enter BILL. *He doesn't see* JANET.

BILL. So this is Maison Claughton . . .

JANET. O — hello.

BILL. Janet, what you doing here?

JANET. My Daddy's house.

BILL. Your old man — Claughton?

JANET. Yes, do you know him?

BILL. Well, no I —

JANET. But what are you doing here Bill . . . ?

BILL. I've err . . . come to mend the telly.

JANET. I thought you were a boxer?

BILL. Bit of a Renaissance man. Turn me hand to anything — or anyone . . .

JANET. O, really . . .

BILL. Don't blush.

JANET. You're blushing.

BILL. It's the light in here. Anyway, oh yes — definitely — your collateral alternator's gone. I'll have to take it back to the shop.

JANET. How did you know it was broken?

BILL. Your old man phoned us up. (*Picks up the TV.*) What you doing tonight?

JANET. Finding Charlie a bed in a hostel.

BILL. Be in touch.

JANET. Hey, can you give me a lift —

BILL. Hurry up then . . .

BILL *goes.* JANET *is about to go.*
CLAUGHTON *enters.*

CLAUGHTON. There is a very important programme on
    television I must watch.

JANET. The man came to mend it and took it away.

CLAUGHTON. Mend it, mend it? There was nothing wrong with it.

JANET. He took it away.

CLAUGHTON. But . . . I want to see the news tonight!

JANET. I've got to dash, daddy. I've got a junkie on my hands.
    (*She goes.*)

CLAUGHTON. Summon the constabulary, my house has been
    burgled.

    Enter SAYERS.

SAYERS. You called, sire?

CLAUGHTON. Someone has stolen my television.

SAYERS. Do you have a description?

CLAUGHTON. 36 inch colour.

SAYERS. Right. And what about the television:

CLAUGHTON. Superintendent.

SAYERS. Sire.

CLAUGHTON. Clearly, enemy forces are at work. Come, let us
    inspect the house's security precautions.

SAYERS (*shouting*). Secure the drawbridge.

    They go briskly.

Scene Eight

Enter VI *with a pram and a bag of washing.*

VI. I do like to watch the washing go round. It makes a nice
    change from the telly. It must be the valium. I get so tense.
    Pete's pining. Pining for my dad. He pines in a peculiar way.
    He has to have it off with barmaids. I don't understand it.
    Funny thing was, when my dad was alive, Pete hated his guts.

She looks at the pram.

Kerry, you miss your dad, don't you. I give him half a valium and he sleeps all right. I love him. I do. But seventeen floors up, and him crawling around . . . I have nightmares about him falling off the balcony. I have to leave the window open. Because the central heating has gone wrong. It's hotter in our flats than it is in the Sahara. Our caretaker said. He reads the temperatures in the Evening News. There's only two hotter places in the world than our flats. We're all on valium, all the women on the 17th floor. I expect that's why I never see no-one. I expect they're all lethargic.

Enter FOX *doing a trick, producing a bunch of flowers.*

O, that's very clever.

FOX. I'm Mr Fox.

VI. I haven't seen you round here before.

FOX. I heard about the incident at your father's funeral the other day. The undertaker told me. He gave me your address.

VI. It was so embarrassing. In the middle of the cemetery. I nearly died.

FOX (*another trick with a cigarette*). Now you see it, now you don't.

VI. That's very clever.

FOX. I imagine Mr Claughton was very angry.

VI. Was he the posh bloke?

FOX. Yes.

VI. He won't pay up the compensation.

FOX. An outrage.

VI. My grandma says he could afford it out of the petty cash.

FOX. He could.

VI. It's very sad.

FOX. I'm a journalist and I'd like to write a story about the . . . outrage.

VI. O, no — you —

FOX. Turn round again. In profile, a striking resemblance.

VI. Eh?

FOX. Never mind. I expect you're tired of being flattered.

VI. I wouldn't go so far as to say that.

FOX. It's just that in profile — your name?

VI. Vi.

FOX. In profile Vi, the way you smile and the way in which you cross your legs — the full voluptuousness of your right thigh.

VI. The other one's just the same.

FOX. I do see a striking resemblance.

VI. Who?

FOX. Angela Rippon.

Pause.

VI. You're having me on.

FOX. Your . . . warmth and natural charm, a sort of glowing sexual intelligence.

VI. Oi, I'll tell my husband of you. (*Slaps him.*) I won't really.

FOX. Especially in your smile. You know how at the end of the Nine O'Clock News, the way she smiles —

VI. They always try to end with a cheerful bit so that she can smile.

FOX. Do smile.

VI. I can't.

FOX. Of course you can.

VI. I've got me curlers in.

FOX. That doesn't prevent you smiling. Go on.

VI. All right. (*She smiles.*)

FOX. Exactly the same! Say, 'The Prime Minister expressed grave concern about the balance of payments.' And smile.

VI. Oooo. The Prime Minister expressed concern about the grave payments balance. (*Smiles.*)

FOX. Trusting, sincere, optimistic. I sense you are a great confidant.

VI. What's that mean?

FOX. You can tell me things I want to know.

VI. If I can . . .

FOX. Vi, I sense you are destined for greater things. Pastures new. I'll be your Svengali.

VI. Watch your language. All I want is a house in Harlow . . . one day.

FOX. You could be where Angela Rippon is.

VI. I went out with the drummer of the Tremeloes once, before I got married of course. And before the Tremeloes made it.

FOX. One trusts Angela Rippon instinctively. Oh yes. She is more than just a face on the television talking about Earthquakes in Romania . . .

VI. Yes . . . ?

FOX. She is a friend in the dark. I switch off the sound sometimes and tell her my problems . . . I sense you can let me do that to you . . . I have a very bad problem. My editor is after my blood. He wants me to find out precisely what happened to Mister Claughton at the funeral.

VI. My contact lenses were steamed up so I couldn't see exactly . . . but I'll take you to see grandma.

FOX. Now?

VI. No. Tomorrow . . . in the gym . . .

FOX. Tomorrow then.

VI. Meet me outside the pram sheds. I don't want the neighbours gossiping.

FOX. Outside the pram sheds tomorrow . . . See you there . . . Angela . . .

She smiles and goes out with the pram doing a high kicking routine.

FOX. Stupid bitch. (*He goes.*)

Scene Nine

Gymnasium. BILL *runs on, training in boxing gloves. Enter* DOC.

DOC. I'm very worried about Vi.

BILL. Have you heard from this Birmingham coon yet? Only a week to the fight — he'll better have his tumble soon.

DOC. Vi's stopped coming to me for valium.

BILL. What? Vi stopped the valium?

DOC. And your grandmother, I'm worried about her. She shouldn't be going on these training runs at her age.

BILL. She'll be here in a minute — the family conference. The council of war —

DOC. Under any other business — my fucking letter.

Enter SAYERS, *in shorts and a bowler hat. He runs on the spot vigorously.*

SAYERS. All right, all right — what's all this about then?

BILL. Me fight.

SAYERS. Not you, something funny is going on. I sense it. I'm watching all you lot, Sprightlys. All the lot of you.

BILL. See you coming a mile off Ronnie, mate.

SAYERS. I fancy not. Master of disguise I am. Should have seen me when I was infiltrating the gang of vicious homosexual murderers. I dressed up in arse crushing tight white jeans and bangles and a poovey hair style. Loitering outside the Trafalgar Square urinals I picked up the esteemed Sir Robert Mark once. He mistook me for a slim hipped sixteen-year-old rent boy.

DOC. Did he hire you?

X's face. *He wears a dinner jacket and a bow tie*

my lords, gentlemen, plebs — at great expense,
her delight the one and only — the sensational,
ob heroine, the pub princess of Hackney — the
ngie Here Is The News Rip 'em off.

Nine O'Clock News theme. Spotlight on VI as
on. She smiles, theme fades. She reads from a

mise over oil prices has been agreed by the 13
ates. According to reliable sources in Kuwait,
e an increase of only 7½ per cent.

usic: Love Potion Number 9. She hurls papers in
gins a dance/strip routine.
e routine, the music stops and she recites a news it

s Ambassador to the United Nations predicts that i
ears before a majority rule settlement is reached in
a. This follows a fact finding tour of Black Africa.

. More music. Strips. Stops.

er union has joined the growing demand for an end t
ial contract. This is the Amalgamated Union of
ering Workers.

n. Music. Now she's down to her knickers.

inally, the weather. Most of Britain will be overcast . .
here are some brighter patches that will reveal themselv
t . . .

emoves her knickers. Ovation. Blackout. Lights up.
and BILL with screen. VI in a dressing gown.
onderful.

SAYERS. Watch it O'Flaherty. We're watching you, and your partner Doctor Popadom.

DOC. Oh my God, like a drink — then you don't mind if I do.

BILL. Do your poovey walk Ronnie — give us a laugh.

SAYERS (*grabs him*). Listen you cocky little sod. I'm onto you. Your rackets, your fiddles. Hasn't it occurred to you that you lot are under my unfailing gaze? That wherever you go, I am there too?

BILL. I thought we must share the same tastes?

SAYERS. No cock ups, Sprightly — no cock ups. Not till my change of beat comes through.

BILL. Change of beat?

DOC. Change of beat?

SAYERS. I am to be promoted. Top national security. So tight lipped is the security, I can't tell even my wife what the new beat is.

DOC. Jesus.

SAYERS (*he does press ups*). So remember, until I take up my new duty, I want you on your best behaviour or I'll jump on you like a ton of hot horse shit. You are my enemy Sprightly. There's an old Arab saying, the Arabs say it all the time in Arab land. The friend of my friend is my . . . (*Pause.*) I'll say that again. The enemy of my enemy is my friend. The friend of my enemy is my enemy. That's what the Arabs say. I was there and heard them saying it. In Arabic. I picked it up, I got the gist of it. So think on it. (*He goes.*)

BILL. Blimey — what's he talking about?

DOC. He says he's got my partner under observation.

BILL. You haven't got a partner.

DOC. And I haven't got me fucking letter.

Enter GRANDMA, breathless, skipping.

BILL. Sit down gran, for Christ's sake take the weight off your pins.

DOC. You're not a young woman anymore Mrs Sprightly.

GRANDMA. Pardon?

DOC. You're not as young as you used to be.

GRANDMA. Brilliant, in't it — what you can work out with a
university education. Well . . . what do we know?

BILL. The social worker girl. She's Claughton's daughter.

GRANDMA. Fucked her yet?

DOC. He came to my surgery —

GRANDMA. And?

DOC. A penile problem. I gave him some Spanish fly. And . . .
endeavoured to spark a positive transferal of his whim for
young girls to . . . a television personality.

GRANDMA. We'll use it.

DOC. How? And get me letter back?

GRANDMA. Vi phoned. There's a journalist bloke coming
who's got it in for Claughton. United, we'll have him.

Enter FOX.

FOX. Hello . . . Vi said I'd find you here. My name is Mr Fox.

GRANDMA. Come in Mister Fox, we've been expecting you.

FOX. I was rather hoping we might help serve each other's
interests.

BILL. Hang about — what do you want out of it?

FOX. O, just a story. I had some rich material on Claughton — but
the lawyers wouldn't let it through.

BILL. How do we know we can trust you?

FOX. What have you got to lose?

DOC. My name's Popadom.

FOX. It's Dr O'Flaherty. Got your letter back?

DOC. O God. Don't mind if I do. (*Drinks.*)

GRANDMA. This Claughton bloke — we're all trained up and

---

roaring to go, bu

FOX (*calls*). Vi, com

VI *enters; she look*

VI. Hello grandma.

GRANDMA. Vi — I har

BILL. I recognise her, b

GRANDMA. You've mad

DOC. I'd fancy her meself
upbringing.

BILL. You've got a plan.

FOX. I've got a plan.

VI. He's got a plan.

DOC. To get me incriminating

GRANDMA. To get Claughton

BILL. To get the twenty grand.

VI. Come on, I'll tell you all abo

She and GRANDMA *go;* BILL

BILL. I'll buy you a drink.

DOC. I don't mind if you do.

FOX *alone does a trick, producin*

FOX. A transformation sure enough
But it's not a joke
Go scoff your ice-creams, have a dr
But do not wander too far away,
In 15 minutes for Claughton we mak
He thinks he'll get a knighthood and
But when our plot begins to spin,
T'will be a different kind of story.

Blackout. Music: Who's Squeezebox by

End of Act One

Interval music from Graham Parker albu

ACT TWO

Scene One

Spotlight on FO

FOX. And now,
for your furt
the heart-thr
incredible A

*Music: BBC
Angela Rip
script.*

VI. A compro
Opec oil s
there will

*Stripper
air and b
During th*

America
will be y
Rhodes

Ovation

VI. Anoth
the soc
Engin

Ovati

And f
but t
tonig

*She
FO*

FOX.

VI. I'm a star, I'm a star.

FOX. They were going wild for you out there. The poor cow doing the Maggie Thatcher strip won't get a look in.

VI. I'm a star, I'm a star. Me eyes are all shiny and normally me tits hurt after running up the stairs when the lift's broken, but now I feel wonderful. I'm world famous in Hackney.

BILL. Have you spotted him?

FOX. He's definitely here.

BILL. He'll be here in a minute Vi.

FOX. He passed a note to the waiter. He said he wants to come backstage and meet you.

VI (*she is putting on stockings*). I owe it all to you Mister Fox. You have shown me how the other half carry on.

FOX. You are the most sensational discovery since Richard Dimbleby swore on television. Fame and fortune are before you, Vi.

VI. All I want is a house in Harlow.

FOX. You shall have fame, fortune and a house in Harlow.

There is a knocking on the floor (off).

BILL. It's him.

FOX. Go and spray yourself with that exotic scent I bought you.

VI. It's so sexy. Just one squirt under me arms and I arouse meself.

BILL. Hurry up.

She goes behind screen. Another knock.

FOX. You know how these tape recorders work?

BILL. Yeah. Press red for record and —

FOX. Make sure the mic's switched on. I'll have the camera behind the screen. Vi, make sure he's facing the screen when you give him the come hither.

She reappears. Agitating her arms.

VI. It's arf stinging. I shouldn't have shaved under me arms.

BILL. What's a little bit of irritation for dad's memory?

Another knock off.

FOX. Come on, before he knocks the door down.

VI. I've never been unfaithful to my husband before . . .

Another knock. FOX *and* BILL *hide behind screen.*

VI. Entrez.

She strikes a seductive pose.
CLAUGHTON enters in evening dress.
Pause.

CLAUGHTON. I just want to say . . . I was deeply moved by
your performance. More moved than even the Bernard Levin
column has moved me.

VI. I don't know what to say. It's the nicest thing anyone has
said to me.

CLAUGHTON. Here, so close to you, you look like a child . . . I
sense chalk dust in your hair and playground scars upon your
knees, your soft, smooth firm, thighs and . . . the very head
girl of my dreams . . . and — (*Sneezes.*)

VI. Bless you.

CLAUGHTON. A fragrance —

VI. Orchid dew.

CLAUGHTON (*sneezes again*). That is most unfortunate. I am
allergic to orchid dew.

VI. I'll scrub it off.

CLAUGHTON. No, that's not necessary . . . it is an allergy that
appeals to the . . . the . . . ahhh tisshooo . . . to the flagellant
in me. Your grasp of world affairs stimulated me.

VI. It's different every day.

CLAUGHTON. You were quite, quite, quite — (*Sneezes.*)

VI. I find it very hard to undo me bra when I have to say Russian
names.

CLAUGHTON. Then allow me to assist you.

VI. You're too kind, sir.

CLAUGHTON. Not yet.

VI. You what?

FOX and BILL's heads appear behind the screen.

CLAUGHTON. I am not a knight of the realm yet.

VI. You're so dignified and responsible . . . you're old enough to be my father.

CLAUGHTON. Not genetically, though perhaps mathematically, ha ha.

VI. I love maths. Aaaah.

CLAUGHTON. Why?

VI. Me armpits are very sore.

CLAUGHTON. Then allow me to lick them better.

VI. Ooo.

He does, then convulsed with sneezing.

CLAUGHTON. Love maths, you say. I have a little mathematical puzzle for you. (*Seductive procedure this.*) A train has 351 passengers at the first station it stops and 16 people get off and seventeen get on and at the next station 19 get off and 31 get on and at the next station 76 get on and 34 get off and at the next station 8 get on and 51 get off —

VI. Yes?

CLAUGHTON. How many stations did the train stop at?

VI. Six.

CLAUGHTON. Fuck it. (*Sneezes uncontrollably.*)

VI. I felt your eyes on me all the time I was performing.

CLAUGHTON. I have never felt so moved by the prospect of continued white supremacy in Rhodesia. (*Another great sneeze.*) This is intolerable, this is impossible. . . (*He goes to go.*)

VI. I'll wash it off.

BILL. Arouse him — say something erotic.

CLAUGHTON. What was that, what was that?

VI. My subconscious talking.

CLAUGHTON. It was a man's voice.

VI. My inner consciousness is masculine. That is why instinctively I know what a man likes.

CLAUGHTON. O, Angela . . . I have tried to fight it off, this throbbing in my groin . . . but I am merely mortal, although I am chairman of a vast consortium and on the Queen's Silver Jubilee Committee.

VI. Blimey George — what a whopper.

CLAUGHTON. Grasp this sceptre of my longing, this regal instrument of ah ah ah ah . . . (*Sneezes.*) Impossible!

VI. No, no don't go — ummm.

FOX. This is the 25th anniversary of the Queen's wedding.

VI. Oh yeah. The Wedding of Princess Elizabeth to Lieutenant Philip Mountbatten brought a day of joy to millions . . .

CLAUGHTON. I was there, I was there . . . I waved my little Union Jack as the Queen passed by . . . I blew kisses at the Queen . . . she wore a gown of supple lamé designed by Norman Hartnell and she carried a bouquet of . . . of . . . of . . .

VI. Orchids?

A great sneeze.

I find talking about the Coronation so arousing . . .

CLAUGHTON. My precious little child . . . let me unburden you of your cares . . .

His trousers fall to his knees as he leaps upon her; a great scuffle — him sneezing and her shouting about her armpits hurting.
FOX *appears and takes flash pictures.*

BILL *appears and holds tape recorder microphone close to them.*
They go to dash off. SAYERS *has entered in a dress and they collide. He has been carrying tape recorder and camera and switches them in collision.*

BILL. Evening darling . . . who are you?

SAYERS. I'm the Margaret Thatcher cabaret.

BILL. What you doing after the show?

SAYERS. Going home in me Panda.

BILL *and* FOX *go.*

Sir . . .

CLAUGHTON. Not yet.

Sees SAYERS. *Leaps up. His trousers are round his ankles and he's wearing Union Jack shorts.*

My God — who did this to my trousers?

VI. You did.

CLAUGHTON. Superintendent . . . allow me to introduce . . .

VI *is about to say who she is:*
CLAUGHTON *slaps a hand over her mouth and in doing so the trousers he had been pulling up fall again.*

This lady is the head of MI5.

SAYERS. I've seen her on the Morecambe and Wise Show reading the news.

CLAUGHTON. The counter espionage nature of the deception fooled our enemies.

SAYERS. I spotted it, but my lips are sealed. Sir, I think it would be best to bid the lady farewell.

CLAUGHTON. Goodbye, my dear . . . goodbye . . .

She goes, blowing him a kiss.

I did not succumb . . . I did not succumb. I didn't even come. I turn my back on vile lust . . .

He has regained composure.

Yes, well Superintendent, everything seems to be in order.

SAYERS. I smell a Sprightly con . . . which by a brilliant stroke of double confusion I have thwarted single handed. (*Raises camera and tape.*) Your every passion throb was recorded, your indiscretion — preserved for posterity and blackmail purposes no doubt. I foxed 'em. Switched the tape recorder with a cassette of Mantovani's greatest hits and bunged 'em a camera full of me aunti Rosie's holiday at Yarmouth.

CLAUGHTON. A magnificent switch. By God — that was close. But . . . (*Pompous now.*) I question your attire —

SAYERS. Permit me to explain. By dressing up in this manner, your enemies will simply assume I'm one of your whores.

CLAUGHTON. Hmm. Superintendent — a word in your ear.

SAYERS. I'll remove my earring.

CLAUGHTON. I think it best, you move into Maison Claughton — an additional security precaution now the countdown to the knighthood has begun.

SAYERS. I doubt that my missus would permit —

CLAUGHTON. Did I tell you how much the Queen approved of your appointment?

SAYERS. The Queen . . . me . . . ? Yes, I think I can move in right away. Wonderful lady, the Queen — and she can ride a horse. When the hour comes to crush the Bolsheviks the union leaders and the nignogs and perverts, she'll lead us from her horse . . .

CLAUGHTON. Side saddle . . .

SAYERS. I'll march behind, chest out, jackboots crushing hippies; plimsolls to right and left — bradishing me truncheon and scraping up the hallowed royal manure for me allotment.

CLAUGHTON. Let us away to Maison Claughton. I'll order a bed for you in the stables.

SAYERS. I'll be on guard at all hours . . . especially at dead of night. The forces of darkness are drawing in . . . there is a shadow spreading across your glorious destiny, I sense it.

CLAUGHTON. I smell your fart.

They go.

Scene Two

Enter BILL, FOX *and* GRANDMA.
BILL *switches on cassette. Mantovani music.*

GRANDMA. Don't sound like the ponce's heavy breathing. What about the camera?

FOX shows a polaroid snap.

FOX. Old lady's face . . .

GRANDMA. Looks like an arsehole with piles.

FOX. We seem to have somehow been . . . foiled.

GRANDMA. It was a foolproof plan. It was guaranteed, you said — put my darling little granddaughter at risk. If she's been fucked in vain —

BILL. Ronnie — he must have done a switch.

FOX. I'm sorry, Mrs Sprightly.

GRANDMA. So you should be.

FOX. So what we'll do is —

Enter VI, *crying, with a pair of black eyes.*

GRANDMA. My gawd, girl — what's the matter with you?

VI. Aw grandma. A terrible thing happened, a travesty of justice happened, the most diabolical thing happened. Pete came back from Canvey Island and he, he —

GRANDMA. He what?

VI. He gave me a mouthful of signet rings.

GRANDMA. That's what I call a diabolical liberty.

VI. He punched me eyes.

BILL. That's terrible.

VI. He really beat me up.

GRANDMA. The wife-bashing bastard — is there no decency in this disgusting world?

FOX. What happened Vi?

VI. See, it was so hot, in the flat, it was really sweltering — according to the caretaker we're hotter than Cairo today . . . When I got back from the . . . you know . . . I got undressed 'cause it was too hot to wear clothes. And I was putting the milk bottles out and he stepped out the lift. He said he'd been pining for me. Then he saw I was starkers and he smelt me smell and he said, 'So this is what happens when I turn me back for five minutes.'

BILL. I'll string him up. I'll pour cement down his dungarees and toss him off Tower Bridge.

FOX. I am sorry Vi.

VI. Thank you Mister Fox. Just as I was discovering me inner self and all.

FOX. It's altogether unfortunate. I was rather depending upon your face being in tip top condition for the Buckingham Palace Garden Party. You see — I wanted you to dress up and impersonate the Queen.

Pause.

VI. The Queen?

BILL. Liz?

GRANDMA. Horsey teeth . . . you mean, her . . .?

FOX. Yes. . .

VI. Oh, I couldn't, I'd die.

BILL. That'd be treason. They still hang you for treason.

FOX. It'll be worth . . . twenty thousand pounds.

Pause.

GRANDMA. Foxy, you've got a plot!

FOX. I had a look the other day at the Royal Mews at Buckingham

Palace. On Wednesdays it's open to the public. Bill and I will visit Claughton as representatives of the Queen. Say she wants to observe him at a little party. A quite natural procedure before the actual knighthood.

GRANDMA. Yes, I see that.

FOX. And also invite him to make a contribution — a personal financial contribution — to the Silver Jubilee Fund. He should hand the money to the Queen personally. To —

BILL. Vi!

VI. Leave off. I can't dress up as the Queen. Not with a crown, not with two black eyes and me teeth knocked out.

BILL. I'll lend you me gumshield and sunglasses.

GRANDMA. Lovely. It'll be all right girl. Really.

VI. Well, all right. But what about me eyes?

FOX. Steak.

VI. Steak? I can't afford steak. But — I've got some beefburgers in the fridge.

GRANDMA. Come on. Let's have a pint and make plans. And that Robertson — I want him as well, class betrayer.

VI, GRANDMA *and* FOX *go.* BILL *is about to follow them off as* DOC *enters.*

DOC. Oi, not so fast now that I've found you. Bill Sprightly right, at last, . . . been looking for you all over. Well?

Pause.

BILL. Well what?

DOC. What about it?

BILL. What about what?

DOC. Exactly. What about what?

BILL. What are you talking about?

DOC. You know what I'm talking about.

BILL. I don't know what you're talking about.

DOC. Listen, I might be stupid, but I'm not Irish. Wait a minute — I might be Irish but I'm not stupid. If you knew me at all, you'd know that I know you know what I'm talking about.

BILL. I dunno what you're talking about —

DOC. Ah yes you do. The fact that you keep not admitting you know proves to me carte blanche that you fucking know. And I know you know. So what about it?

BILL. You're pissed.

DOC. I'm not pissed. I haven't had a drop all day. Not since this morning when I drank someone's urine sample they'd stupidly put in a Jamesons' bottle.

BILL *laughs.*

I suppose you think that's funny.

BILL *laughs more.*

It's not bloody funny. And I tell you something else that's not funny, shall I?

He grabs BILL.

What about me letter?

BILL. What letter?

DOC. Jasus — you've forgotten about the letter?

BILL. What letter?

DOC. My letter. The letter I wrote Harry that they found. The incriminating, devastating, career-ruining letter that I wrote for you and never even got paid for!

BILL. Don't worry about — we've got a plan.

DOC. You've got a plan — good lad, I knew you wouldn't let me down. So everything's under control. Excellent — want a drop, don't mind if I do. What exactly is the plan?

Pause.

You double dealing bastard; you haven't got a plan. You've left me to fate. After all I've done for you. Giving Claughton aphrodisiacs and all. Right then Billy boy — I leave you to your fate, too.

BILL. You what?

DOC. You'll see, you'll see. I'm not telling you. 'Cause I've forgotten about it. I've forgotten all about it.

BILL. Forgotten about what?

DOC. O it's difficult now, in't it. You seem to forget I hold the whip hand. What about Winston Kershaw?

BILL. What about Winston Kershaw?

DOC. The dumb nignog boxer you wanted to take a tumble before the fight at Shoreditch.

BILL. You've written the note?

DOC. No, I've not written the note.

BILL. For Christ's sake, the fight's on June 1st.

DOC (*triumphant*). I know, I know. O I bloody know all right.

BILL. Well then —

DOC. You'll get no more notes from me. You'll have to have the fight, Billy boy, you cocky sod.

BILL. He'll kill me — it's out of the question. No way, no way.

DOC. Serves you bloody right.

BILL. Doc, please.

DOC. You'll have to go sick yourself — and get some other mug doctor to write your letter, not me, oh no.

BILL. I can't go sick again. The double dealing nigger. Doc please. I'm too young to die — too beautiful to get duffed up.

DOC. I've got you by the short and curlies. Winston Kershaw's called your bluff. You're on your own Sprightly. I'll get the letter back without your help. And you'll have the fight without mine!

DOC *goes out laughing.*

BILL. Wednesday June 1st. It'll be a sell-out at Shoreditch Town Hall. Air heavy with cigar smoke, gloves on, the clinking of glasses, the clanging of the bell and the chattering of teeth. Mine.

He dashes off.

Scene Three

CHARLIE *staggers on playing the trombone badly.* JANET *sets up a tennis ball on elastic game and begins to play.*

JANET. Wonderful.

CHARLIE. I'm crap. This is a very beautiful garden of your father's. But it's the wrong ambience for playing the horn.

JANET. It sounds wonderful — why don't you have a little rest?

CHARLIE. Oh yeah . . . I'm terrible now.

JANET. No, no, no — don't be self-defeating. It really moved me Charlie. I mean, to be quite frank, I don't know much about music. To tell you the truth I'm tone deaf as well as colour blind. But I tell you in all honesty I'm doing my best for you.

CHARLIE. Janet because you're so nice to me I'll tell you the truth. I never really had it.

Pause.

JANET. Had what?

CHARLIE. The horn, I never really had it. I always wanted to play alto sax. That was the trouble. I dug Charlie Parker — he could blow. When I was 23 and had saved up enough money for an alto sax, I went in the shop to buy it and bought a trombone instead.

JANET. How sad. Didn't they have any alto saxes?

CHARLIE. They had dozens. But Ra told me to buy a trombone.

JANET. Ra?

CHARLIE. His voice spoke to me. He's an ancient Egyptian sun god. He talks to me a lot when I drop acid. Have you noticed, you can't get any good acid now. Like Sardos. That's very pure. My shrink gets it for me —

JANET. You never told me you had a psychiatrist —

CHARLIE. I gave him up. He wanted to get me into an asylum. I wasn't having that. Those places are full of lunatics.

JANET. You should see him — he'll be able to cope with you much better than me.

CHARLIE. I went to him after all the success of the Dusty Springfield disc. I mean, I found it really hard to cope with all that success.

JANET. Please Charlie — you really shouldn't keep coming here . . . I must have some retreat where I can retreat to.

She has bent to pick up the ball. Her arse is in the air and BILL *enters and gropes her exposed buttocks.*

Daddy!

BILL. You what?

JANET. Oh Bill — what are you doing here?

BILL. Janet, I've got a present for you.

JANET. Oooh, what is it?

BILL. Some sexy silk lingerie, look. (*Opens bag.*)

JANET. Beautiful . . . beautiful. There's a laundry label on the —

BILL (*ripping it off*). A little joke. A present in return for your help.

JANET. My help?

BILL. Janet — your old man, has he got such a thing as . . . a morning suit?

JANET. A morning suit?

BILL. See, I can't even afford to hire one — all the expense I went to buying you the sexy gear there.

JANET. When do you need it?

BILL. Right away.

JANET. You must be about his size . . . hang on . . .

She goes to go. BILL *sees* CHARLIE.

BILL. You bastard — you crooked class betraying pimp —

He dashes at CHARLIE *and forces him to the ground.*

CHARLIE. Hey —

JANET. Bill, Bill — what on earth —

BILL. Calls himself a union official —

JANET. He never calls himself a union official —

BILL. I'm not surprised, you hypocritical bastard.

JANET. Charlie, get up.

BILL. I'm very surprised you mix with such scum.

JANET. Poor Charlie, he does no harm. All he wants is to —

CHARLIE. I think you think I'm my brother.

Pause.

A lot of people think we look alike. He's very straight, I'm very bent. If I grew taller I'd be a circle. Harr. That's one of Ra's little jokes. In the morning he's full of laughter. I woke up and he made me laugh for hours this morning. I just laughed and he laughed and laughed — (*Shakes goonishly.*)

BILL. I ain't fucking surprised. (*Coughs.*) Sorry — technical hitch, I though you were . . . never mind.

JANET. Well . . . at least you've met. Bill's my boyfriend. Bill, be nice to Charlie, he's very worried about June 1st.

She goes, blowing a kiss to BILL.

BILL. Did she say, you're very worried about June 1st.

CHARLIE. On Wednesday I'm playing horn for the new Sex Pistols single.

BILL. Well, I'll be buggered, what a coincidence.

CHARLIE. Err —

BILL. I was chatting away to Johnny Rotten only half an hour ago.

CHARLIE. You know Johnny?

BILL. Yeah, I know this wholesaler who gets him the safety pins for his ear'oles cut price.

CHARLIE. I'm very worried about the gig.

BILL. O, it'll be great — the atmosphere of that place.

CHARLIE. Olympia studios hasn't got any atmosphere.

BILL. That's why they changed the venue.

CHARLIE. I didn't know.

BILL. Then it's a good job we've met up Charlie mate. Nar, they decided they wanted a place with a bit of atmosphere, a bit of heat, a bit of bloody life. Same date, June 1st — in the evening — great place, Shoreditch Town Hall.

CHARLIE. Shoreditch Town Hall?

BILL. Just arrive about seven o'clock, mention my name — Bill Sprightly and you'll have a . . . great time, a real knock out.

CHARLIE. I'm glad I met you. Or I'd have gone to the wrong place.

Enter JANET.

JANET. I say, you two seem to be getting along famously. Here's the suit — daddy never wears it since mummy ran off with Eugene. (*Hands the morning suit to* BILL.)

CHARLIE. You know something Janet — your boyfriend is a real friend. He's restored my confidence.

JANET. Wonderful —

CHARLIE. I'll go blow a bit . . .

He staggers about.

JANET. Bill, I just want to say —

BILL. I'd better be off, Jan gal.

JANET. You're so kind. You're exactly the sort of person who hides his deep sensitivity behind an aggressive exterior, aren't you.

BILL. Gotta go and help a couple of old ladies across the road. Thanks for the whistle —

BILL *goes.*

JANET. He's a wonderful man.

CHARLIE. He is . . . He's kinda . . . inspired me. I'm gonna find out about the landlord who put me in the gutter.

JANET. The name of the landlord'll be on the rent book.

CHARLIE. Yeah — Claughton Investments.

JANET. What?

CHARLIE. That's the bastard's name . . .

He staggers off as JANET *reels.*

JANET. Are my ears deceiving me? Can it be true? It's not possible. Daddy wouldn't do such a thing . . . oh God . . .

A golf ball rolls to stage centre, followed by CLAUGHTON *with golf gear.*

CLAUGHTON. Not a bad shot, and not a great shot. If I had been aiming for the lawn instead of the 15th green perhaps two hundred yards away I'd have been tolerably pleased.

JANET. Daddy — how could you do it?

CLAUGHTON. Sliced my shot.

JANET. Pull down a man's home when he went to buy a tin of Brasso for his trombone.

CLAUGHTON. You are talking in riddles child — be quiet.

JANET. I am not going to be quiet. My most problematic client is . . . a victim of your savage property company.

CLAUGHTON. The price of progress. Now silence, I say. I didn't send you to Benenden to have you raise your voice against mine.

JANET. Daddy, I implore you —

CLAUGHTON. Superintendent —

Enter SAYERS *peering all about him through binoculars, still in drag.*

JANET. Voyeur.

CLAUGHTON. This is Superintendent Sayers of the Flying Squad.

JANET. So it's true what they say about the Sweeny.

CLAUGHTON. Escort Madam Mao to her room.

JANET. I am quite capable of going myself. I wouldn't dream of breathing the same air as you. You might charge me a percentage.

She stomps off.

CLAUGHTON. She's like her mother. Guttersniping when she knows my nerves are on edge. (*Tosses the club in anger.*) Damn blast. (*Pause.*) I miss her mother . . .

SAYERS. I know, sire. I can tell.

CLAUGHTON. It's a beautiful evening . . . smell summer coming in across the rose trees . . . and the twilight . . . night-scented stock and a haze of gnats hovering above the lily pond, like incense. You know superintendent, in the half light . . . you look not . . . not wholly unlike . . . my wife . . .

SAYERS. Thank you, sire.

CLAUGHTON. When she was younger. Her hips were slim, like yours. (*Feels his hips.*) We used to sit here, as the sun went down on a summer evening . . . she used to kiss my ear . . . poke her tongue in it and . . . kiss it . . . (*Giggles.*) I wonder who's kissing her ear now . . . (*Giggles.*) Are your ears ticklish, superintendent?

SAYERS. Err . . . well . . . ar . . .

CLAUGHTON. This is how she went . . .
SAYERS. Aaah.

CLAUGHTON. Nice isn't it.

SAYERS. Well, I wouldn't . . .

CLAUGHTON. I like your dress —

SAYERS. Laura Ashley . . .

CLAUGHTON. I haven't touched a woman for . . . days now . . . but I am a mortal man. I like the warmth of a kindred spirit in my bed. (*Pause.*) I feel you are . . . a kindred spirit, superintendent . . .

SAYERS. I'm a married superintendent, sire.

CLAUGHTON. I won't tell anyone . . .

SAYERS. Sire . . . what if we are being observed . . . through radar antennae, bouncing it off satellites to Peking?

CLAUGHTON. Your skin is so young . . . I sense playground scars on your knees and hockey stick bruises upon your ankles . . . let me lick away your cares.

In embrace they fall to the floor. They both leap up, as the trombone blows off.

Good God, pull yourself together Claughton. Down vile erection, down. Forgive me, Sayers.

SAYERS. I, too, have pranged the torrid heat of passion.

CLAUGHTON. What has come over me — the damned doctor's passion killers are the very lust bubblers of my ruin lest I . . . (*Roars.*) A fortnight has passed since the Buckingham Palace phonecall. And not one word. Where is my knighthood? I demand my knighthood? (*Stamps feet and goes.*)

SAYERS. Sod this for a game of soldiers. But I sense a mortgage in the offering. I can sense it.

SAYERS *goes.*

Scene Four

Enter ROBERTSON, *packing a briefcase.*

ROBERTSON. All this bloody bumf. Transport House just keeps churning it out. All right for them. They just write it, they don't have to read it. I haven't seen The Sweeny for a fortnight and as for Hughie Greene . . . I said to my son, all right you're a bloody Trot, but — but — cut out the jargon, cut out the statistics, cut out the high faluting theory and what have you got? What have you lot of Trots got to offer, eh? O that foxed him — that kept him quiet for a good minute and a half. Then out it all poured . . . I was happier when he used to wank over Vanessa Redgrave.

Enter GRANDMA, *smartly dressed with a heavy veil on her hat hiding her face. She has a script; she sometimes reads from it.*

GRANDMA. Can I come in?

ROBERTSON. Robertson the name. District organiser.

GRANDMA. I wish to speak to you in confidence about an official matter.

ROBERTSON. Well, we're not bugged here, as far as I know.

GRANDMA (*reading the script*). Mister Robertson — your services to our nation have not gone unchartered.

ROBERTSON. Been talking to the wife have you, ah ha ha.

GRANDMA. You'll be aware that this year is Her Majesty the Queen's Silver Jubilee.

ROBERTSON. Yerrs, now you come to mention it, I do believe I've seen something or other about it.

GRANDMA. The Queen has drawn up a special honours list of personal selections to celebrate the festivities. Your name has been appended as a deserving beneficiary of an OBE.

ROBERTSON. Well, blow me down — that must be Derek at head office!

GRANDMA. I am not at liberty to say.

ROBERTSON. Well well well . . . I'll not deny I've worked my damnedest for more years than I care to recall . . .

GRANDMA. I call on you as a representative of Her Majesty . . . and I simply ask you whether you will consider accepting her award.

ROBERTSON. Haven't I seen you somewhere before?

GRANDMA. I'm on the newsreels when Lizzie's there — I'm her handmaiden. Well?

ROBERTSON. Well, what can I say? Oh yes, I'll consider it . . . I don't see how the acceptance of a non-monetary honour can in any way be . . . err . . . construed as a betrayal of my class.

GRANDMA. You accept then?

ROBERTSON. I do.

GRANDMA. Such is the protoco . . . protoc . . . What's that fucking word? (*Shows him the script.*)

ROBERTSON. Protocol.

GRANDMA. Such is the protocol of my visit, I am not able to accept your acceptance.

Pause.

ROBERTSON. I wonder, perhaps, clarification here.

GRANDMA. If you are willing to accept the honour, you must call at the Royal Mews beside Buckingham Palace tomorrow morning, at eleven o'clock.

ROBERTSON. Tomorrow morning, well — I was due to look into this containerisation wrangle at Islington but —

GRANDMA. The Queen will receive you tomorrow morning. At 11.00.

ROBERTSON. In the Royal Mews —

GRANDMA. One other matter. It is a very informal occasion. The Queen has decided . . . to encourage the joyous festivity, that tomorrow her guests should attend in fancy dress . . .

ROBERTSON. What a splendid idea!

GRANDMA. Here is your costume. An admiral of the fleet . . .

She hands him a suitcase.

ROBERTSON. Ha ha. O splendid. We seem to have sorted out all this without animosity or rancour. Good-day your ladyship.

She goes.

ROBERTSON (*calling after her*). Still got me Coronation mug, you know. Handle fell off 15 years ago, but I've still got it. I'd better shoot round and tell Lil, and her mum — Lady from Buckhouse called. They're going to bung me a gong!

He goes.
Night.

Just a safe illuminated. Sound of a window opening, dogs barking. In creeps DOC. *Then the window crashes down. In bursts* SAYERS *in a woman's nightdress, brandishing a chair as a weapon.*

SAYERS. Stop — in the name of the law.

DOC. Jesus Christ. You probably wonder what I'm doing in here.

SAYERS. Is that a trick question? Hang on — I've heard that one before. No good, right — give me a clue.

DOC. I'm looking for a golf ball.

SAYERS. A golf ball?

DOC. It came in, through the window.

SAYERS. But the window is closed.

DOC. It came in so fast, the amazing thing was — the ball didn't break the window.

SAYERS. That's impossible — I know for a fact that that fact is not a fact.

DOC. That's what I said to Mister Claughton.

SAYERS. You are playing golf with Mister Claughton?

DOC. Correct.

SAYERS. Now wait a minute, it's midnight — pitch black darkness.

DOC. That's perfectly true . . . only time to get the course to oneself, not many people think of playing at midnight.

SAYERS. Too dark to see —

DOC. An illuminous golf ball. It was Mister Claughton's idea.

SAYERS. He's a genius.

DOC. Indeed. 'Twas he who spotted the ball pass through the window into the study here.

SAYERS. How very observant of him.

DOC. He explained that such was the speed of the ball and on account of the darkness, so unprepared was the window that it didn't have time to react in the way that windows normally react when struck by a heavy object travelling at great speed. It must be here somewhere . . .

SAYERS. Now wait a minute, wait a minute — that's Mister Claughton's private safe of private and highly confidential reports and papers. I can't stand here and let you rummage through it.

DOC. Then sit down.

SAYERS. Even I, his most entrusted confidant do not know the combination of that lock.

DOC is holding a stethoscope to the safe.

DOC. Then you'd better sit down and I'll blindfold you in case you are ever tortured for the information — that way you can honestly tell them you do not know.

SAYERS. A first class precaution.

DOC. Say you were blindfolded and bound to a chair.

He blindfolds him and binds him to a chair.

SAYERS. Like these vicious homosexual murderers, these slim hipped Adonises of rent boys who bind and gag their victims before rummaging through their safes and stealing —

He's gagged. DOC opens the safe.

DOC. O God, what am I doing? Where's me fucking incriminating letter?

JANET enters in pyjamas.

JANET. Daddy, I thought I heard you. I just want to say goodbye.

DOC (*muffled voice*). Goodbye. (*Keeps his back to her.*)

JANET. Aren't you going to ask me where I'm going?

DOC. Where are you going?

JANET. I've taken an overdose. I'm killing myself.

DOC. You what?

JANET. Daddy I can't bear it, the stigma — the irony. Me working 200 hour weeks coping, trying to help the debris of the nuclear family problem — the casualties you create. I've taken those sleeping pills that doctor gave you . . . I've taken them all and I feel . . . strangely . . .

DOC (*turns*). You took all the aphrodisiacs I gave your old man?

JANET. You're not daddy, My God — I feel so randy — you beautiful hunk of manhood you —

She leaps upon him.

Going to rape you, you're going to impale me —

DOC. Help, for God's sake, help me, help me.

They roll on the floor.
Enter CLAUGHTON in a dressing gown.

CLAUGHTON. What in the name of God is going on?

Looks.

Janet, enough is normally enough. But now enough is too much.

JANET. I'm all wet for you . . . and I'm dying.

CLAUGHTON. Explain yourself first. Without doubt, this is the work of some maniacal prankster.

Escaping from JANET, DOC collides with CLAUGHTON.

Doctor Popadom. What are you doing here at this hour?

DOC. Feeding the horses.

CLAUGHTON. Janet, I cannot endure the excrutiating embarrassment of your presence. Pack your bag immediately.

She picks up DOC and goes screaming, carrying DOC in a fireman's lift.

CLAUGHTON (*ungagging him*). And now Superintendent, Mastermind — perhaps you will endeavour to explain this . . . this . . .

SAYERS. Then I shall endeavour to explain. On the night in question I was proceeding in a North Westerly direction up the east wing of Maison Claughton when I did hear —

Enter BILL and FOX, both dressed in morning suits and wearing sunglasses.

BILL. Good evening, forgive the lateness of the hour. We wish to speak to Horace Claughton.

SAYERS. I'll deal with this . . . Right, who are you and what is your business and don't give me none of that don't say nothing till I've spoken to me solicitor or I'll have your guts for garters.

BILL. A confidential matter.

SAYERS. Speak now or forever hold your peace.

BILL. We are emissaries from the Palace.

SAYERS. What Palace?

CLAUGHTON. Silence, you half wit.

FOX. Buckingham Palace.

SAYERS. A trick question that was.

The sound of banging and screams (off).

CLAUGHTON. Damned girl. Excuse me a minute. Silence child.

CLAUGHTON *goes out.*

SAYERS. Can you prove your assertion?

BILL. Here is my card.

SAYERS. But this is a tourist picture postcard of Buckingham Palace.

FOX. The Queen is on an economy drive.

SAYERS. Just testing. (*Inspects it as though it were a forged bank note.*) Yes, I can say without a shadow of a doubt it does appear to be a quite genuine picture postcard of Buckhouse.

CLAUGHTON *enters.*

CLAUGHTON. A little trouble with my daughter. Ammonia works wonders, ha ha. Glass of sherry?

SAYERS. I can assure you sire, they are from the Palace.

CLAUGHTON. Excellent, at last — Destiny calls.

BILL. We wish to speak to you privately —

SAYERS. Haven't I seen you somewhere before?

CLAUGHTON. I hardly think you mix with emissaries of our Gracious Majesty the Queen.

SAYERS. Adjust your dress, sire.

CLAUGHTON. Yes, ah.

BILL. Since our business is highly confidential — would you ask Mrs Claughton to leave us alone?

CLAUGHTON. Ah, actually this is —

FOX (*flashbulb pops, his camera*). Security. We need a photograph of your wife so that at the gates of the Palace when the two of you arrive the guards will recognise her as your wife. You read between the lines?

Pause.

CLAUGHTON. Excuse me my dear . . .

SAYERS. Of course, darling.

They kiss and SAYERS *goes.*

FOX. I'm delighted to note such warmth and affection between you. You'll know full well a happy and secure marriage is an essential pre-requisite for a knighthood.

CLAUGHTON. Absolutely. As you witnessed, I qualify on that point.

FOX. There could be no knighthood without your good lady at your side.

CLAUGHTON. Quite quite. Get on with it.

BILL. Before the actual honour may be bestowed upon you. Her Majesty has decided upon a slight change of protocol — a new innovation for the Silver Jubilee.

CLAUGHTON. What is it?

FOX. Intended recipients are required to attend a social function so that they might be observed under Her Majesty's gaze. Tomorrow morning, 11 o'clock, a little soirée at the Royal Mews — do bring . . . Lady Claughton . . .

CLAUGHTON. Ah, what an excellent idea, how regally informal, how splendid. Just that . . . I seem to have mislaid my morning suit somewhere and — not much time to get a replacement.

BILL. Never mind my dear fellow . . . you can borrow mine.

CLAUGHTON. I couldn't dream of accepting a loan of —

BILL. Let's say twenty quid.

CLAUGHTON (*hands him money*). Done.

FOX. So anxious is Her Majesty to ensure all feel wholly relaxed and at ease, she thought tomorrow should be a fancy dress party.

CLAUGHTON. I see.

FOX. She has selected for you . . . this costume.

Removes Mother Goose costume from bag.

CLAUGHTON. Well, perhaps someone more worthy would prefer such a splendid costume . . .

BILL. You are very favoured.

CLAUGHTON. Needn't have paid you £20 for the morning suit.

FOX. It's an Old Mother Goose costume.

CLAUGHTON. Yes, I do see that.

BILL. As a child, Old Mother Goose was always the Queen's favourite pantomime.

CLAUGHTON. Really, fascinating. But is it absolutely necessary?

FOX. Are you declining?

CLAUGHTON. No, whatever gave you that idea?

FOX. There is one other matter —

CLAUGHTON. Are you sure we haven't met before?

FOX. At a Sandringham dinner party?

CLAUGHTON. That must be it, yes, yes. Wonderful pheasants.

FOX. Before the actual honour can be bestowed, some gesture of loyalty to the Royal Family is required.

CLAUGHTON. My loyalty has never been called into question.

FOX. Such has been the enormous financial strains placed upon the Royal Family's personal fortunes in organising the many festivities this year —

CLAUGHTON. I know, I know — I'm on the committee damn it.

FOX. That a financial gesture is deemed appropriate. Twenty thousand pounds.

Long pause.

CLAUGHTON. I thought, for one dreadful moment then . . . a slight aberration, a malfunctioning of my ears, perhaps, overcome by the emotion of your visit, for one moment I thought you said . . . twenty thousand pounds.

BILL. Not a penny more.

FOX. Twenty thousand?

BILL. In used bank notes.

CLAUGHTON. But, but but.

BILL. That's the deal.

CLAUGHTON. I see. My only reservation is that it might not seem, should word slip out, perhaps this . . . donation . . . might be incorrectly construed as in effect tantamount to purchasing a knighthood. (*Laughs unsurely.*)

FOX. That's a treasonable assertion.

CLAUGHTON. Quite, forgive me, forgive me. (*He falls to his knees holding the Mother Goose head.*)

BILL. What'll happen is this. So no-one notices, so word don't slip out — the Queen will come up to you tomorrow morning in the Royal Mews and she'll say . . .

CLAUGHTON. What?

BILL. A code word.

CLAUGHTON. Yes?

BILL. She'll say, Nice One Cyril. Then you'll slip her the money and she'll hide it under her tiara.

CLAUGHTON. In used bank notes?

BILL. That's it.

CLAUGHTON. I see.

BILL. Goodnight . . . sir.

FOX. Until the morning, goodnight, sir —

They go.

CLAUGHTON. But the morning suit . . . the twenty pounds —

But they've gone.
CLAUGHTON still on his knees.
Spectacular golden lights.
Fade in music: Land of Hope and Glory. It increases in volume throughout the speech.

CLAUGHTON. Your Majesty, our beloved and worshipped sovereign, whom God preserve, most excellent Majesty, sovereign of the United Kingdom of Great Britain and Northern Ireland and other realms and territories Queen. Head of the beloved Commonwealth, Defender of the Faith, sovereign of the British order of knighthood, and sovereign head of the order of St John, Lord High Admiral, Captain general of the Royal Regiment of artillery, Colonel-in-Chief of the Life Guards, the Royal Scots Greys Dragoons, the Green Jackets, the Royal Tank Regiment, the Southern Highlanders, the Royal Rhodesian Rifles, the Sierra Leone Military Forces, the Canadian Navy and the Ottawa Mounties, Master of the Fishing Fleets, Head of the National Hospital Services Reserve, Field Marshal of the New Zealand Engineer Corps, the Queen's Own Cameron . . . Cameron Highlanders, the Trinidad and Tobago Wireless Operators Regiment, Air Marshal in Chief of the Nairobi Fire Service, Supreme Head of the Church of England and all who sail in her baptism fonts, I your humble, humble servant Horace Randolph Claughton adorn myself with this sacred crown, kneeling hunched in blessed servitude . . .

Scene Five

Blackout. GRANDMA *reading aloud from Playgirl.* BILL *with her in a morning suit.*

GRANDMA. He let out a shrill gasp as he writhed in his taut leather jockstrap — his wrists and ankles bound by firm metal chains to the bedposts. He heard her tearing at her plastic mac and felt the thud of soft cream buns splattering against his Wellington boots. This is it he thought as she leapt upon him —

Laughs.

This is what's in store for Claughton after we've taken him to the cleaners.

BILL. One thing at a time, gran. Christ, this collar is bleeding strangling me.

GRANDMA. Where are the others? Bert'll be here in a minute with the ice-cream van.

BILL. We going in that?

GRANDMA. We all gotta get there together.

BILL. Look nice that, turning up at Buckingham Palace in a bleeding ice cream van.

GRANDMA. I suppose Claughton'll go in his Rolls.

BILL. He's taking the cop, dressed up as his wife.

GRANDMA. Vi should be here by now. I hope them black eyes have gone down a bit.

BILL. All she's gotta do is say 'nice one Cyril' is his ear'ole and he'll toss her the twenty grand.

GRANDMA. Then you toss it to me, I'll toss it to Bert and him and me can speed off down the Mall — in the ice cream van.

Enter VI *and* FOX.

GRANDMA. You all ready then Vi?

VI. Under me coat. I'll put the crown on when I get in the ice cream van.

GRANDMA. Let's have a look at your eyes — O, they're much better.

They begin to go as JANET *enters on her bike. She wears a gymslip.*

JANET. Hello everybody.

GRANDMA. We're in a hurry ducks.

JANET. Goodness Vi, what's up?

VI. Walked into a lamppost.

FOX. Her husband beat her up.

JANET. How thrilling!

BILL. You what?

JANET. Oh Bill, you're so hung up. You're just not in touch with your body at all.

BILL. Eh?

GRANDMA. Excuse us, love. Why don't you go for a long walk.

JANET. Yes, I must. To the Buckingham Palace Royal Mews. One of my old Benenden friends rang me up — she's a handmaiden to the Queen now and she invited me along to the Mews to see the horses and the wonderful thing is, one of them is foaling and the Queen herself will be there at eleven thirty. Must dash, toodaloo.

She cycles off.

BILL. Bloody hell.

GRANDMA. O no.

VI. The Queen there . . . we can't . . . we daren't.

FOX. Now wait a minute, it's all arranged. The Queen won't be there till eleven thirty — that gives us half an hour. Come on.

Pause.

GRANDMA. For Harry . . . Hackney . . . and our twenty grand!

They go.

Scene Six

Trumpet fanfare. GUARD *marches on.*
SAYERS *enters, looks around, whistles and on waggles*
CLAUGHTON *as Mother Goose.*

SAYERS. We're here.

CLAUGHTON. I'm suffocating.

SAYERS. Ah, he's a guard — he'll be in charge. Psst.

GUARD. Madam?

SAYERS. I am not a woman.

GUARD. No madam.

SAYERS. I am Superintendent Sayers of the Flying Squad.

GUARD. I couldn't agree more madam.

SAYERS. My warrant card.

GUARD. In your bra?

SAYERS. This is the Royal Mews?

GUARD. Feel free to wander. It's open to the public. Every Wednesday morning.

SAYERS. Not this Wednesday, I fancy. With the Queen in attendance.

GUARD. It's all this walkabout cobblers. Close to the public, informality.

SAYERS. Not so informal as to disregard security precautions. What are they?

GUARD. Hundred per cent.

SAYERS. Fine, now tell me — what will the queen be dressed up as?

GUARD. Eh?

SAYERS. It's a fancy dress party for God's sake. Didn't anyone tell you that? Then why do you think he's dressed as a goose and me as Barbara Cartland?

GUARD. I thought you was both mad.

CLAUGHTON. Where is the Queen? The Queen has summoned me, the Queen wants me, I am here to be observed under a relaxed and informal gaze. I am relaxed and informal.

GUARD. Entrez, please do.

CLAUGHTON. Oh yes . . .

SAYERS. This way your royal excellency . . .

They enter and pace.
JANET arrives on her bike.

JANET. Whoops.

GUARD. No school parties today miss.

JANET. Janet, Hackney Crisis Intervention.

GUARD. Oh yerrs?

JANET. I'm not a schoolgirl, Good Lord no — put this old Benenden gear on, a little surprise — reunion with old Gob Stopper Gertie.

GUARD. Gob Stopper Gertie, oh her — the Queen's handmaiden who loves horses, none the less.

JANET. That's her.

GUARD. Haven't seen her. But do feel free —

JANET. Thanks, bungho. (*She cycles round.*)

SAYERS. Could that be the Queen?

CLAUGHTON. On a bike? She hardly has a regal air and yet . . . there is something about the gentle rolling movement of her buttocks in those flannel drawers that arouses in me, an emotion . . . ahhhhh.

SAYERS. Steady on sir — Mother Goose, not Rip Van Winkle.

CLAUGHTON. Down vile thing, down vile thing, down . . .

SAYERS. She is looking at you . . .

CLAUGHTON. I am being observed . . . (*Loud voice.*) Yes, I started the company pretty much from scratch, now it's worth at a rough estimate, pre-taxed profits, thirteen million —

ROBERTSON *arrives in the admiral's costume.*

ROBERTSON. Robertson the name, district organiser of —

GUARD. Wander freely.

ROBERTSON. Very civil of you, just want to water the old greens, point percy at the regal porcelain. Where could I pay a call of nature?

GUARD. Between you me and the gatepost, the horse trough over there.

ROBERTSON. Much obliged.

He enters.

SAYERS. Look over there, look over there — Prince Philip!

CLAUGHTON. Looks younger than he does on television, and hardly what you might call a regal air.

SAYERS. He is a Kraut after all. Six years of war fighting the Jerries and she goes and bloody marries one.

CLAUGHTON. Greek.

SAYERS. It's all Greek to me.

ROBERTSON. I recognise your voice — Mister Claughton, we've met before.

CLAUGHTON. Ah yes, I imagine we move pretty much in the same social whirl. Oh yes, quite quite. I'm pretty much a self made man but I sent my daughter to Benenden —

ROBERTSON. Anne's school —

CLAUGHTON. Yes indeed! Wonderful place here, splendid, quite splendid.

ROBERTSON. Not bad is it. Nice now the old sun's out.

CLAUGHTON. Where, I haven't seen him yet?

ROBERTSON. Up there.

CLAUGHTON. Oh what, flying eh? Ha ha. I wasn't blessed with a son.

ROBERTSON. Eh?

CLAUGHTON. You must be awfully proud of your son.

ROBERTSON. Tell you the truth, I'm bloody disgusted with him.

CLAUGHTON. Really, you surprise me.

ROBERTSON. Difficult sod. Always rowing. Always about politics. Gets on her tits. She turns up the volume of the telly.

CLAUGHTON. Good Lord.

ROBERTSON. Oh yerrs, right embarrassment to me in my job.

CLAUGHTON. I find that astonishing.

ROBERTSON. Stands to reason. Me in my position with a son who's — he's a bloody Trotskyite.

CLAUGHTON. Good God. I had no idea.

ROBERTSON. All he talks about is the bloody revolution.

CLAUGHTON. Well, lots of youngsters nowadays do.

ROBERTSON. What I say to him is this — right, how are you going to get twenty five million workers to follow you?

CLAUGHTON. Tell him, he can count on me, I'll be there.

SAYERS. So will I.

ROBERTSON. Nice having met you again. I'm going for a piss in the horse trough. Don't tell Liz.

He goes.

SAYERS. I'd better report this to MI5 — Prince Charles a Trot.

CLAUGHTON. Wonderful chap, Philip. I'm going for a piss in the horse trough — don't tell Liz. He said. There's an anecdote for the Club. Yes, old Philip said to me, just going to have a piss in the horse trough, harr harr. Then he said, don't tell Liz. Wonderful, oh this is what I was born for. Exchanging bon mots with the Royal Family, ah yes.

VI, FOX *and* BILL *enter. She wears a crown and sunglasses.*

BILL. Now you know what to do?

FOX. Face me, drag him round, so I can snap it all.

VI. Yes.

BILL. Sooner we do it, sooner we're away . . .

SAYERS. Sir, sir — look.

CLAUGHTON. Yes, yes — the very Lady of the Camellias of my dreams. . .

BILL. Mister Claughton, allow me to introduce —

CLAUGHTON. Your Majesty . . . I am unworthy to stand on the same earth as you. I bow before you (*He kneels.*) I have instructed my tailor to sew magnets to my shoulders so there shall be no slip.

VI. Nice one Cyril. (*She drops her bubble gum.*)

CLAUGHTON. Your majesty, permit me to pick up your bubble gum . . . there.

She sticks it on the side of her crown.

VI. Tar, nice one Cyril.

CLAUGHTON. Beautiful spectacles —

BILL. Sun makes her eyes water —

CLAUGHTON. Yes, yes, your husband mentioned the unfortunate political stance Charles has taken, but just a passing phase I'm sure . . .

VI. Nice one Cyril.

CLAUGHTON. Oh yes — you've met my wife? Here dear, the attaché case . . .

BILL. Open it, let's see it's all there.

CLAUGHTON. By all means . . .

Opens case to show VI. *Flashbulb pops.*

CLAUGHTON. Ah, staff photographer. Perhaps you can send me a few hundred copies, for friends and business acquaintances. Where the devil has she gone? Your Majesty — you've forgotten to tap me shoulders.

VI *and* BILL *take the money and go.*
CLAUGHTON *is still on his knees.*
Trumpet fanfare.

GUARD. Be upstanding — Her Majesty The Queen.

First bars of God Save The Queen.
Enter ELIZABETH *in stable clothes.*

ELIZABETH. So kind, so kind.

CLAUGHTON. Who the devil is that woman? In such scruffy clothes — she looks like a stable char at some backstreet gymkhana.

SAYERS. Hello hello — my senses are sensing. Could this be the terrorists about to strike?

ELIZABETH. So kind, so kind.

CLAUGHTON. Where's my good friend Philip — he'd never allow such plebs in here.

ELIZABETH. So kind, so kind.

CLAUGHTON. Where is the Queen, where is the Queen —

FOX. Why, here is the Queen.

ELIZABETH. So kind, so kind —

CLAUGHTON. Silence madam, will you stop that boring cliché. Where is the Queen?

ELIZABETH. I am the Queen.

CLAUGHTON. Oh quite. Quite. Anymore Queens of England here?

ELIZABETH. I am the Queen of England.

CLAUGHTON. If I were you madam, I should be very quiet. To claim such rank is nothing short of treason.

ELIZABETH. Who are you?

CLAUGHTON. I am Horace Claughton.

ELIZABETH. Ah, your name I know from the Silver Jubilee Fund in Chislehurst, isn't it?

CLAUGHTON. And district, yes . . . Do you mind. Take your filthy hands off my costume —

ELIZABETH. Only horse shit —

CLAUGHTON. I do not want horse shit on my costume. Away vile imposter.

GUARD. Take your wings off the Queen.

CLAUGHTON. This is not the Queen. I have already met the Queen. I picked up her bubble gum.

ELIZABETH. Bubble gum?

SAYERS. A word in your ear, sire. This lady would under close inspection appear to be . . . the Queen.

CLAUGHTON. Her most excellent majesty . . .

ELIZABETH. Sovereign of the United Kingdom of Great Britain and Northern Ireland and other realms and territories, sovereign of the British order of knighthood —

CLAUGHTON. My God, you are the Queen! Well, what about my knighthood? (*Kneels before her.*)

ELIZABETH. We do not knight geese.

CLAUGHTON. O, this preposterous costume. (*Begins to take it off.*)

ELIZABETH. You are hardly behaving in a manner fit to —

CLAUGHTON. Behaving perfectly well enough for you to take me twenty grand in used bank notes.

ELIZABETH. What?

CLAUGHTON. Your lady in waiting took them.

ELIZABETH. What, Gob Stopper Gertie?

CLAUGHTON. In sunglasses and a Cockney whine.

ELIZABETH. Are you suggesting I would accept payment from you?

CLAUGHTON. Well, just before Philip went for a piss in the horse trough —

ELIZABETH. Guard, arrest this man. Send him to The Tower.

CLAUGHTON (*now stripped to his Union Jack underpants*). Curious logic that. Trots in the Royal Family and —

ELIZABETH. I don't know what you're talking about.

CLAUGHTON (*as* GUARD *holds him*). Your son, the heir to the throne is a Trotskyite!

ELIZABETH. Off with his head.

ROBERTSON (*entering*). Your excellent majesty — how about me gong?

CLAUGHTON. Ah, Philip —

ROBERTSON *looks all around for Philip.* FOX *is photographing all this from a safe distance.*

Philip, you told me Charlie was a Trot —

Enter JANET.

JANET. Charlie here?

CLAUGHTON. Up there Philip said —

JANET. Smashed again.

ELIZABETH. Janet, isn't it? In Anne's form at school. I haven't seen you since the last hockey match.

JANET. Gosh, your majesty. I didn't think you'd recall me.

ELIZABETH. Do come and see the new foal. Heard the good news? About to become a granny.

ELIZABETH *and* JANET *go. The* GUARD *is leading* CLAUGHTON *in the opposite direction.*

CLAUGHTON. Janet, Janet — wait, please, it's me, daddy. Get these people off me Janet.

ROBERTSON (*running off after Queen*). Your Majesty, what about me OBE?

CLAUGHTON. I've been duped, aaaahhhh. (FOX *photographs him.*) You, I thought I recognised you. You shithouse.

FOX *goes out laughing.* CLAUGHTON *is being led off.*

Your majesty, do not forsake me. Trembling here in me underpants before you. As deserving a knighthood as any bent arsed politicians, embezzling lawyers, pot smoking pop singers and Ena Sharples in her curlers — please, please.

He and the GUARD *are gone.*
SAYERS *alone picks up the discarded costume.*

SAYERS. Perfectly good mortgage gone up the spout and no mistake.

He goes.

Scene Seven

Night. Wind in trees. A dog barks. A church clock strikes two. Then, very beautiful and haunting — an alto sax plays a verse of You Don't Have To Say You Love Me.
JANET *enters with suitcases. She stops and listens.*

JANET. Charlie . . . Charlie . . . where are you . . . what are you doing here at two o'clock in the morning . . . where are you?

CHARLIE *staggers out of the darkness with alto sax. He has black eyes and a bloodied face.*

Charlie . . . your face . . . what's happened?

CHARLIE. I got . . . beaten up . . . I went to the gig, and the man said come in and . . . I mentioned your boyfriend's name and the next minute some spade was punching me . . . they gave me a hundred quid . . . I bought an alto sax. I don't like the Sex Pistols now . . .

JANET. That sounded beautiful . . .

CHARLIE. The beating kinda cleared my head . . .

Pause.

JANET. I'm going away Charlie . . . I'm leaving Crisis Intervention . . . I've achieved nothing. I can't cope anymore.

CHARLIE. I'm sorry . . . thank you for trying to help me.

JANET. There's a minicab waiting — can I drop you off at home?

CHARLIE. I don't have a home . . . he took it . . . the man who lives here . . . . . he took my home and everything I won . . . I bought a cutlass Janet . . . I'm going to skin him . . .

JANET. No you're not . . . come —

CHARLIE. Don't try and stop me Janet . . .

The cutlass flashes in the moonlight.

JANET. Don't Charlie . . . there's no point. He's beaten . . . finished . . . throw it away.

Pause, then CHARLIE *drops it.*

JANET. Come blow for me!

They go hand in hand.
CLAUGHTON *enters carrying a shotgun.*

CLAUGHTON. Janet, Janet — wait, please, I need your help —

Sound of a car (off) starting and driving away.

Janet . . . gone. Dearest wife . . . gone . . . laughing stock . . . traitor . . . retrograde . . . social vagabond . . . an outcast . . . a lunatic.

Makes lunatic noises.

Not a Royal Garden party . . . a mad hatter's tea party . . . and twenty thousand pounds gone . . . paid for the humiliation . . .

He puts the gun in his mouth.
SAYERS *enters in Act One suit and a bowler hat.*

SAYERS. Mister Claughton — don't.

CLAUGHTON. Why? Give me one good reason.

SAYERS. I'd be up before the commissioner and lose me pension.

CLAUGHTON. Protect me, protect me — you led me head first into the pandemonium.

SAYERS. How was I to know it was all topsy turvy and not as it seemed. I have never trod such hallowed regal lawns before.

CLAUGHTON. You berk. If I hadn't put my trust in you I would never be in this . . . irretrievable, hopeless position. I have no alternative but to kill myself. I am a man of honour.

SAYERS. You're the first person to appear half naked in public before a reigning monarch for six hundred years.

CLAUGHTON. I shall blow my head into the sky . . . all is lost.

SAYERS. Sshh, what's that?

They listen, SAYERS *flashes a torch.*

In the bushes . . . a rustling noise . . .

CLAUGHTON. Who's there . . . Janet . . . are you back . . . or my dear wife . . . returned in the hour I most need her love?

Out of the darkness steps GRANDMA, *laughing.*

SAYERS. Old ma Sprightly — the architect of your downfall.

GRANDMA. Go on, kill yourself you old shithouse. Not that you've the nerve. Have to be a man to kill yourself. You're not a man, you're a two legged rat with a knob on.

CLAUGHTON. Gloating at my ruin. Why, why ruin me, why destroy me?

GRANDMA. Giving you a taste of your own medicine — showing what it's like to be on the receiving end.

CLAUGHTON. For what reason?

GRANDMA. 'Cause you, all of you — you dish it out without thinking . . . crush us into the ground — you contemptible ponce. Go on, go on kill yerself — put yourself out of our misery.

CLAUGHTON. I have a gun in my hand. I could kill you.

GRANDMA. You wouldn't kill no-one, 'cause you ain't got the nerve. You might get your hands dirty. Look me in the eyes Claughton — remember me. Just a nothing, but brought you tumbling —

The gun explodes. GRANDMA *drops dead. Deathly silence.*

CLAUGHTON. What . . . what . . . she taunted me. She deserved it . . . Aaaaaah. I killed her . . . but, but, in self defence . . . this sword from my hall, it was in her hand . . . she tried to attack me, that's why I shot her.

SAYERS *has put the cutlass in* GRANDMA's *hand.*
ROBERTSON *enters, in a trilby, smoking a pipe.*

ROBERTSON. But I saw exactly what happened Mister Claughton.

CLAUGHTON. What?

ROBERTSON. You buggered up my chances of getting a gong, you nasty bastard.

SAYERS. Queen don't give gongs to junkies.

ROBERTSON. You're confusing me with my identical twin —

SAYERS *shoots him dead.*

SAYERS. Pervert. England's better off without him.

CLAUGHTON. You fool. You fool.

SAYERS. Not quite a fool. I took the precaution of wearing gloves, Mister Claughton. Your finger prints on the gun.

CLAUGHTON. They'll think I . . . shot them both . . .

SAYERS. Then that explains everything . . . A shooting accident. Something moved in the bushes while shooting grouse . . . fired, you did . . . two bodies discovered. The remorse of the terrible tragedy . . . led to your unnatural behaviour before the Queen. A quite understandable breakdown.

CLAUGHTON. That with the Queen happened yesterday — I shot them tonight . . .

SAYERS. There is a doctor I know who specialises in mistaken certificates . . . I summoned him to certify you've had a breakdown. Ah, here he is . . .

Enter DOC.

SAYERS. I'd like to introduce you, Mister Claughton, Doctor O'Flaherty.

CLAUGHTON. I've met your partner, Doctor —

DOC. Chapati.

CLAUGHTON. Popadom.

DOC. Poppycock.

SAYERS. Doctor here has a request to make. He would like you to destroy a letter he wrote about Harold Sprightly.

DOC. Yes . . .

CLAUGHTON. That case, the correspondence is all in my files.

SAYERS. I'll see the good doctor to your study. In return for
the Harold Sprightly letter, he'll write out two death
certificates and date them yesterday.

CLAUGHTON. Very well.

    SAYERS *gestures* DOC *off.* DOC *goes.*

SAYERS. Then, might I suggest a short holiday? Bahamas or
something? Then everything back to normal. The nation needs
you. A strong leader.

    Pause. CLAUGHTON *begins to go, pausing at* GRANDMA's
body.

CLAUGHTON. They went to all this trouble . . . two deaths . . .
for a mere twenty thousand pounds? I shall attend their
funerals. And offer my deepest condolences.

    He goes.

Scene Eight

SAYERS *remains on stage as* VI, BILL, FOX *and* DOC *enter with
wreaths. Church bell chimes slowly.*

VI. A new doctor put me back on both the valium and the librium.
I take the valium in the morning and the librium at night,
and honest, now I'm so lethargic I can't even watch the Nine
O'clock News. The Mogadon helps me sleep. Goodbye
grandma.

BILL. I was going to start a little business with my share of the
twenty thousand. But the police reclaimed the money.
Claughton had marked the notes. Goodbye grandma.

SAYERS. The money Claughton gave me. A reward. Commissioner
called me in his office after I handed in my report. Instructed
me to take a rest which I am now enjoying in the comfort of
my mortgageless mock Tudor mansion in the wog-free suburbs.

Great life it is too. Only trouble, they won't let me join the golf club. Committee's full of bloody Yids.

DOC. It took a bit of time to convince the undertaker of time of death since rigor mortis hadn't yet set in. But I opened the Jamesons and he didn't mind if he did. I'm on two bottles a day now. The new practice is next to the Chislehurst girls convent school, you see.

VI. Goodbye, grandma.

FOX. I wrote it, the story of the decade. But my proprietor killed it, he thought it was too embarrassing to the Queen. He's after a knighthood you see. It looked good set up, before he destroyed the copy, the photographs and negatives. Ah well. I thought I might have exposed Claughton. Perhaps when he stands at the by-election. They adopted him last week.

He produces a bunch of flowers.

Grandma Sprightly lies beneath this tree
Died celebrating the Silver Jubilee
She tried to take on the upper class
Now the worms are gnawing at her arse.

He drops the flowers on her body.
Blackout. Music loud: Graham Parker's That's What They All Say.

End of play.

Appendix

Changes made for Des McAnuff's production at the St. Laurence Centre for the Arts, Toronto, Canada, January 1980. (See Author's Note.)

Throughout: for *Queen's Silver Jubilee* substitute *Queen's Royal Oil Year Festival;* for *Angela Rippon* substitute *Margaret Thatcher;* for *VI's dream of Harlow home* substitute *emigrating to Canada.*

Page 1: Before the play begins, insert:

Music: The Beatles' 'Money' and 'God Save The Queen'.

Prologue

as spoke by Mr. Fox

Across the Atlantic to an oil slick stinking sea,
Malicious and corrupt behind its pageantry,
A journey we shall make to the city of London,
Distinguished are its villains; the poor are undone,
Worship is of wealth and power over people,
Only the dead are spared scandal and evil,
Royal Brittania! Unlike the French, the queen gives no cake,
Let them have a festival — to disguise the bankrupt fake,
Dulled by strikes, greed, despair and all that shit,
Many are deceived; but the wise exploit it,
Yesteryear the Silver Jubilee was a lucrative cheat,
More festivals were suggested to camouflage defeat,
A reason was needed to arrest more Turmoil,
So what better cause than to celebrate oil?
The North Sea fields made Britain self-sufficient,
Elizabeth Regina gave the celebration her royal assent,
Royal Oil Year 1980 they call it — for no special reason,
Save it is the start of a decade — and another season of treason.

He magically produces a Union Jack, flourishes it and vanishes in a cloud of green smoke.

Page 1 line 2: stage direction before first speech, omit:
as lights go up on Hackney Marshes, Sunday Morning, very early.

Page 4 line 18: for VI's speech 'When we get the money . . .
a house in Harlow.' substitute the following:

VI. When we get the money, all our dreams will come true. We'll
pay off the HP, get off the Bad Debtors list and they said:
Then Canada will welcome us with open arms. It's a wonderful
new start, that country. I know: my Auntie Nell said before
she died. She would have died years before but for the fresh
air and carefree life in Alberta.

Page 9 line 15: after 'what this country needs is someone to
look up to': insert the following:

'No disrespect intended to the ladies, but a woman as Prime
Minister! I mean, one thing them running the homemade cake
stalls at church bunnions. But it's another thing when it
comes to running the country. And a great country — self-
sufficient in oil this year. Be reasonable! Can you see Hair
Lacquer Thatcher head of fucking OPEC? Dishing out orders
to Shake-Your-Camel-Turds and similar smelly Arabs? We
need a strong man to stop all this . . . '

The speech carries on with 'weak kneed nancy pancying pussy
footing' etc (line 17).

Page 20 line 23: for VI's speech 'I'm thinking, if dad had got
the money . . . with an integral garage.' substitute the following:

VI. I'm thinking how dad would have used the money to pay off
our debts. A very nice man at Canada House said they'd
welcome me and Pete and Kerry with open arms if we paid
off our debts and Peter never mentioned his criminal record.
Pete's skilled. Even the man at Canada House said Pete's
calibre of electronic expertise was wasted on blowing up
jeweller's safes. He said Canada was very go ahead. Pete said
on the application form he was a security examiner.

The scene resumes with the stage direction '*Enter* CHARLIE,
staggering etc.'

Page 33 line 11: FOX'S monologue 'Incest in suburbia? . . . I'll
fill my seven columns every day.' was cut and instead he danced
and did a series of increasingly spectacular conjuring tricks to
Joe Jackson's song *Sunday Papers*.

Page 37 line 6: after the stage direction 'CLAUGHTON *enters*' insert the following: '*He knocks down a patient on crutches, bound entirely in bandages.*' The scene resumes with CLAUGHTON's speech 'I demand to see a doctor.' etc. (line 7).

Page 39 lines 12-19: omit these lines and substitute the following:

DOC. Find inspiration in a national figure whom you can admire for his utter ruthlessness. What you must do is transfer your irrational lust to a being out of your reach. Is there anyone you especially admire in politics?

CLAUGHTON. All the great statesmen are dead . . . except! (*His face is full of joy.*)

DOC. Who? What man inspires you?

CLAUGHTON. The greatest Englishman alive. Our beloved Prime Minister — blessed Margaret Thatcher.

DOC. Good God! Another woman —

CLAUGHTON. A woman amongst women!

DOC. Certainly the loudest speaking.

The scene resumes with CLAUGHTON's speech 'You have been very helpful, Doctor.' (line 20).

Page 39 line 25: after the stage direction 'CLAUGHTON *goes handing the doctor a £20 note.*' insert the following: '*On his way out he again knocks over the patient on crutches who has spent the entire scene regaining his stance.*' The direction resumes with 'DOC *swigs frenziedly at the flask.*' etc. (line 25).

Page 44 line 8 — page 45 line 19: omit Angela Rippon dialogue between FOX and VI and substitute the following:

FOX. When you look serious, the similarity is extraordinary. Say something in a posh voice.

VI. I can't — I can't. I've got me curlers in.

FOX. Margaret Thatcher speaks in the same voice when she wears curlers.

VI. She sounds as though they're arf hurting.

FOX. Say something like her. Go on.

VI. How?

FOX. Imagine you're constipated. And shouting at a very backward negro child on a windy day. That's the voice.

VI. Like this?

FOX. Yes — that's it.

VI. She always smiles a lot. (*Smiles.*)

FOX. Keep smiling . . . say . . .

VI. What?

FOX. Say: 'There are no conservative plans to introduce euthanasia for old age pensioners in order to control inflation. Instead we shall reduce their pensions and ban them from all food shops.'

VI. There are no conservative plans to introduce euthanasia for old age pensioners in order to control inflation. Instead we shall reduce their pensions and ban them from all food shops.

FOX. Vi, I sense you are destined for greater things. Pastures new. I'll be your Svengali.

VI. Watch your language.

FOX. One trusts Margaret Thatcher instinctively. She is a friend in the dark. I switch off the sound sometimes and tell her my problems . . . I sense you can let me do that to you . . .

The scene resumes here (line 21) until Fox's speech (line 32) where 'Margaret' should be substituted for 'Angela'.

Page 49 line 29: the interval music at the end of Act One should be changed to Nick Lowe's *Born Fighter*.

Page 50: after Act Two and before Scene One insert the following stage direction: *Blackout, fanfare. Followed by audience background noises.*

Page 50 lines 1-26: omit these lines and substitute the following:

Spotlight on FOX's *face. He wears a dinner jacket and a bow tie.*

FOX. And now, my lords, gentlemen, plebs — at great expense,

for your further delight, the one and only — the sensational,
the heart-throb heroine, the pub princess of Hackney (*Drum
roll.*) the incredible Maggie 'The Cat' Thatcher.

*T.V. political programme theme music. Spotlight on VI as
Maggie Thatcher. She smiles. She reads from a script.*

Good evening. And believe me, it is a good evening. Of course,
there will be some who say: 'O no. It's a dreadful evening.'
But the moaners aren't going to contaminate us anymore with
their catalogues of woe and misery and communism. Because
the vast majority said: 'Enough is too much.' They said it's
time to put the G back into Great Britain. Get it up. Get
industry going. And above all — Let's be proud there's a G
in Great Britain. Although, I understand in some parts of
the Commonwealth, they call us the United Kingdom. Well,
let's not split hairs. It may not have a G — but it jolly well
ought to.

Stripper music. She strips. Stops.

Incentives — that's what makes a great country. And there's
no incentive to be healthy when the health service is free.
So *that's* why we must put additional charges on medicines
and hospital beds. Some say they're too expensive — well, I
believe medical treatment is worth spending money on. And
if some can't be bothered to pay — well, they don't really
deserve to remain healthy. There were too many hospitals —
it encouraged people to stop work at the slightest excuse —
anything from an appendicitis to a brain haemorrhage. Last
year, do you know how many days were lost through so-called
sickness? It's not as though the hospitals weren't open after
work hours.

'Bump and Grind' music. She strips further. Music stops.

Unemployment numbers *will* decrease: there's won't be so
many people left to be unemployed. Inflation will fall:
prices must get to a level out of the reach of all but those
who have the breeding and education to appreciate expensive
items. It's going to happen all right.
I don't shiver at the thought of what lies ahead. I'm not fearful

of the mighty thrust to fruition. I believe I shall feel satisfied at the end of the day.

To use a cricket term (and don't forget ladies play cricket, ha ha) if we keep a straight bat and no silly mid-offs, we'll reach our goal and sprint over the marathon ahead and I promise you, you'll see the bright patch that's been hidden far too long. Let's do it together: let's have a go. Let's put the G where it belongs.

She removes the G-string. Ovation. Blackout.

Page 51 line 3: for 'strip' substitute 'belly-dance'.

Page 51 line 17: for 'house in Harlow' substitute 'little home on the prairie'.

Page 52 line 31: for 'say Russian names' substitute 'quote the new unemployment figures.

Page 55 line 7: for I'm the Margaret Thatcher cabaret.' substitute 'I'm the Barbara Cartland floor-show.'

Methuen's Theatre Classics

English and foreign classic plays from the Greeks to 1914 with a particular appeal to modern readers and playgoers. The translations are modern acting versions proved in performance and each volume carries a full introduction usually with a chronology of the author's life and work.

Buchner	DANTON'S DEATH *(English version by James Maxwell; introduced by Martin Esslin)* WOYZECK *(translated by John Mackendrick; introduced by Michael Patterson)*
Chekhov	THE CHERRY ORCHARD *(translated and introduced by Michael Frayn)* UNCLE VANYA *(translated by Pam Gems; introduced by Edward Braun)*
Euripides	THE BACCHAE *(English version by Wole Soyinka)*
Goethe	IRONHAND *(adapted by John Arden)*
Gogol	THE GOVERNMENT INSPECTOR *(translated by Kitty Hunter-Blair and Jeremy Brooks; introduced by Edward Braun)*
Gorky	ENEMIES THE LOWER DEPTHS *(translated by Kitty Hunter-Blair and Jeremy Brooks; introduced by Edward Braun*
Granville Barker	THE MADRAS HOUSE *(introduced by Margery Morgan)*
Hauptmann	THE WEAVERS *(translated by Frank Marcus)*
Ibsen	BRAND A DOLL'S HOUSE AN ENEMY OF THE PEOPLE GHOSTS PEER GYNT *(translated and introduced by Michael Meyer)*
Jarry	THE UBU PLAYS *(translated by Cyril Connolly and Simon Watson-Taylor; edited by Simon Watson-Taylor*
Molnar	THE GUARDSMAN *(translated and introduced by Frank Marcus)*
Synge	THE PLAYBOY OF THE WESTERN WORLD *(introduced by T. R. Henn)*
Tolstoy	THE FRUITS OF ENLIGHTENMENT *(translated and introduced by Michael Frayn)*
Wedekind	SPRING AWAKENING *(translated by Edward Bond; introduced by Edward Bond and Elisabeth Bond)*
Wilde	THE IMPORTANCE OF BEING EARNEST *(introduced by Adeline Hartcup)* LADY WINDEMERE'S FAN *(introduced by Hesketh Pearson)*
Anon	LADY PRECIOUS STREAM *(adapted by S. I. Hsiung from a sequence of traditional Chinese plays)*

Standard editions of the plays of many of the leading writers of
Britain, Ireland, Europe and America.

Jean Anouilh	ANTIGONE
	BECKET
	THE LARK
John Arden	ARMSTRONG'S LAST GOODNIGHT
	PEARL
	SERJEANT MUSGRAVE'S DANCE
	THE WORKHOUSE DONKEY
John Arden and	THE BUSINESS OF GOOD GOVERNMENT
Margaretta D'Arcy	THE HERO RISES UP
	THE ISLAND OF THE MIGHTY
	THE ROYAL PARDON
Wolfgang Bauer	SHAKESPEARE THE SADIST and other
and others	plays including:
	Bauer SHAKESPEARE THE SADIST;
	Rainer Werner Fassbinder BREMEN COFFEE;
	Peter Handke MY FOOT MY TUTOR;
	Franz Xaver Kroetz STALLERHOF
Brendan Behan	THE HOSTAGE
	THE QUARE FELLOW
	RICHARD'S CORK LEG
Edward Bond	BINGO
	THE BUNDLE
	THE FOOL & WE COME TO THE RIVER
	LEAR
	NARROW ROAD TO THE DEEP NORTH
	THE POPE'S WEDDING
	SAVED
	THE SEA
	THEATRE POEMS AND SONGS
	THE WOMAN
John Bowen	LITTLE BOXES
Bertolt Brecht	BAAL
	THE CAUCASIAN CHALK CIRCLE
	THE DAYS OF THE COMMUNE
	THE GOOD PERSON OF SZECHWAN
	THE LIFE OF GALILEO
	MAN EQUALS MAN & THE ELEPHANT CALF
	THE MEASURES TAKEN and other Lehrstücke
	THE MESSINGKAUF DIALOGUES
	THE MOTHER
	MOTHER COURAGE AND HER CHILDREN
	MR PUNTILA AND HIS MAN MATTI
	THE RESISTIBLE RISE OF ARTURO UI
	A RESPECTABLE WEDDING and other
	one-act plays

	THE RISE AND FALL OF THE CITY OF
	MAHAGONNY & THE SEVEN DEADLY SINS
	SAINT JOAN OF THE STOCKYARDS
	THE THREEPENNY OPERA
Howard Brenton	THE CHURCHILL PLAY
	EPSOM DOWNS
	MAGNIFICENCE
	PLAYS FOR THE POOR THEATRE
	THE ROMANS IN BRITAIN
	WEAPONS OF HAPPINESS
Howard Brenton	BRASSNECK
and David Hare	
Mikhail Bulgakov	THE WHITE GUARD
Shelagh Delaney	THE LION IN LOVE
	A TASTE OF HONEY
David Edgar	DESTINY
	MARY BARNES
Michael Frayn	ALPHABETICAL ORDER &
	DONKEYS' YEARS
	CLOUDS
	MAKE AND BREAK
Max Frisch	ANDORRA
	THE FIRE RAISERS
Jean Giraudoux	TIGER AT THE GATES
Simon Gray	BUTLEY
	CLOSE OF PLAY & PIG IN A POKE
	DOG DAYS
	OTHERWISE ENGAGED and other plays
	THE REAR COLUMN and other plays
	STAGE STRUCK
Peter Handke	KASPAR
	OFFENDING THE AUDIENCE &
	SELF-ACCUSATION
	THE RIDE ACROSS LAKE CONSTANCE
	THEY ARE DYING OUT
Barrie Keeffe	BARBARIANS (KILLING TIME; ABIDE
	WITH ME; IN THE CITY)
	GIMME SHELTER
	(GEM; GOTCHA; GETAWAY)
	A MAD WORLD, MY MASTERS
Arthur Kopit	INDIANS
	WINGS
David Mercer	AFTER HAGGERTY
	THE BANKRUPT and other plays
	COUSIN VLADIMIR &
	SHOOTING THE CHANDELIER
	DUCK SONG
	HUGGY BEAR and other plays
	THE MONSTER OF KARLOVY VARY &
	THEN AND NOW